(62 - 16318)

THE MASSACRE OF SAINT BARTHOLOMEW

THE MASSACRE OF SAINT BARTHOLOMEW

by Henri Noguères

Translated by Claire Eliane Engel

THE MACMILLAN COMPANY · NEW YORK

A DIVISION OF THE CROWELL-COLLIER PUBLISHING COMPANY

This translation © GEORGE ALLEN & UNWIN LTD 1962

Translated from the French
LA SAINT BARTHELEMY
© EDITIONS ROBERT LAFFONT, 1959

Library of Congress catalog card number: 62-16318

Printed in the United States of America

FOREWORD

This book might have begun, without any preamble, with the sentence: 'It happened on Sunday, August 24, 1572 . . .' But in passing back over four centuries, it is rather difficult to step into everyday life in such a casual way, for things then were so very different from what they are now. It is even more difficult if the event to be described, far from being an everyday episode, is set against a political, diplomatic, philosophical and social background of uncommon complexity.

Consequently, before describing the hours, and often the minutes which elapsed immediately before the fateful night and day of St Bartholomew, 1572, we feel a compelling need to introduce the reader to the leading characters and their setting, and the main aspects of the drama which will be enacted before him at such a speed that there will be no time to glance backwards.

As for the drama itself, we shall endeavour to get the chief characters to describe it in their own words. But among witnesses called to give evidence at a trial which has not always been fair, how many are we going to find who are both direct and impartial? Was there even one who really looked at contemporary events with cold objectivity and recorded them without omitting their most important aspects, perhaps even because of an unreliable memory? Some were carried away by hatred and others by a craving for revenge; others, to look more important, deliberately exaggerated their own parts, or from fear glossed over their own activities. Finally, there were some who, either in flattery or treachery, laid special stress on the attitudes of their leaders.

For the modern reader, the sum of such widely differing behaviour or involvement contains a large number of contradictions; but luckily, these have scarcely any effect upon the main aspects. They can be detected when trying to piece the facts together, and when, checking them hour by hour, or even minute by minute, inaccurate statements are found which cannot always be explained by mere lapses of memory.

Such inaccuracies or contradictions may not simply be ignored, nor may they be over-exaggerated, even if it is obvious that their authors are biased. So we are going to run through the whole list of witnesses, kings, middle-class men, princes of the Church of Rome, pastors of the Reformed Church, captains and workmen. They are all going to tell their tales and often contradict one another. Some of them relate what they have seen, or what they thought they saw, or often what they wanted to see on that day of days.

And then the reader will be left to decide what sort of truth emerges from it all.

CONTENTS

ILLUSTRATIONS

The Stifling Summer of 1572

PARIS was in a wretched temper.

First of all, it was too hot. Day after day, while the dark clouds piled up, the people of Paris were longing for the storm which would bring at least an illusion of coolness. But it was indeed only an illusion, for when sometimes in the evening the clouds burst and let fall a slight shower, the dust in the street was hardly damped by the few heavy drops, and from it rose a steamy heat and a suffocating stench.

A storm was brewing in men's spirits as well as in the air.

There were no newspapers, nor anything like the *avvisi* that kept the Venetians informed of what was taking place in their Republic and in the world at large. Nevertheless, every evening the citizens of Paris discussed the news that passed from mouth to mouth and was carried usually by the beggars, pedlars, or thieves who, from morning till night, idled around the Louvre and sometimes succeeded in worming their way into the court-yard of the palace, slipping past the dozing Swiss guards and mixing with the passers-by, visitors or courtiers who thronged there.

The people of Paris did not like what they heard. Paris was a Catholic city, not merely by tradition, habit, or even laziness, like several other big cities in the kingdom of France, but because its faith had the violent, brutal gregariousness which Paris can evince on the occasion of serious political crises. Such was the case in that stifling summer of 1572: it was brought about, not so much by discussions on religious dogma as by international intrigue, clan rivalries and personal hatreds aroused during earlier religious wars.

The Scriptures and the Church

Hardly fifty years had elapsed since the German monk, Martin Luther, had begun his struggle against the formidable structure of the Roman Chuch. Luther had sought for and, according to him, actually found, the Way of Salvation through direct converse with God, who spoke to him through the Scriptures. As he had refused to put the Church above the Scriptures, he had been cast out as a heretic. Excommunicated and outlawed, Luther, a formidable polemist, had then dedicated his life to teaching a doctrine which found an immense audience, since the whole of Christendom had been aroused and enlightened by the Humanists, the need for a spiritual reformation corresponding to the intellectual and artistic Renaissance.

It was scarcely thirty-six years since a Frenchman, Jean Cauvin, known as Calvin, emerged with a new message and published the first edition of his *Institutes of Christian Religion* in Basle, thus giving fresh sustenance to Protestant propaganda and opening a new path to the Reformation.

And only thirty-one years earlier, a Spanish nobleman, Ignazio de Loyola, who had been for a short time Calvin's school-fellow at Montaigu College in Paris, had been elected— *ad majorem gloriam Dei !*—first general of the Society of Jesus, the Jesuits.

Such a short span of years had been enough to turn the whole of Europe, Catholic for so many centuries, into a battlefield. The Reformation and the Counter-Reformation were locked in a bloody and pitiless struggle in which the gallows answered the stake, and cavalry the arquebusiers. The first wave of the Reformation had submerged Germany, as Luther had thought only of preaching to his own countrymen. Then Lutheranism quickly gained possession of Northern Europe, conquering Scandinavia, and had begun, with some difficulty, to find a foothold in Eastern Europe. The Reformation had thus found stability with this first Lutheran phase. It made a fresh outburst some twenty years later with the new impetus from Calvin, an equally impressive move, even more deadly to Rome by reason of its new trend towards universality.

Calvin was a humanist, while Luther, in his arguments with Erasmus, actually reviled scholarship. Calvin was as much a citizen of the world as a Frenchman could be, while Luther never completely got beyond the mental state of a German pastor. Calvin was a lawyer and a statesman as well as a theologian, and he did organize a state as well as a church. He succeeded in driving a strong wedge into the positions of the Roman Church in countries in which Luther had convinced only a handful of scholars, who had paid for it with their lives. Calvinism was stolidly entrenched in its Genevese fastness and was looking to new conquests: Britain, the Netherlands and France.

Only two countries had remained impregnable to the successive assaults of the Reformation: Italy and Spain, where the Inquisition had come into action at once with merciless fury and where the Society of Jesus had organized a cunning, constructive counter-offensive.

Such is the very rough outline of the whole situation. But the people of Paris in 1572 did not care a rap about how Protestantism was spreading over the map of Europe. So far as foreign affairs were concerned, their ideas were more precise and summary. They could be summed up in a few names, often mentioned in conversation; persons of first importance like Philip II of Spain, Queen Elizabeth of England, Mary Queen of Scots, and the Pope.

His Catholic Majesty

Less than one year earlier the Spanish fleet had won an overwhelming victory over the galleys of Selim II the Drunkard, the pitiful successor of Soliman the Magnificent. A hundred Turkish ships—on which, alas! Christian slaves were chained as rowers —were sent to the bottom. One hundred and three galleys were taken captive into Italian harbours by the victor, the youthful Admiral, Don Juan of Austria, the King of Spain's bastard brother. Forty thousand infidels were sent to Allah's paradise. The tremendous impression made upon the whole of Christendom by this unparalleled naval victory had not yet faded. The King of Spain had reaped such prestige that he had become the unquestioned defender of the faith. Moreover, Philip II, whose staunchest support—even as far as the West Indies—was the Inquisition, which was eradicating in Spain the last signs of Moorish occupation, knew no better title than that of 'His Catholic Majesty'. Although the son of Charles V was only forty-five, he had been discharging the most exacting political responsibilities for over thirty years.

He was hardly more than a boy when his father had placed in his hands the regency of the Kingdoms of Castile and Aragon, not merely in title, but with all the attributes of sovereignty. At the same time, he was married to a Portuguese Infanta of his own age: no private life was more tied to public duties than his.

Ten years later, a widower for the first time, Philip embarked for England with a fleet of seventy vessels to marry his aunt, Mary Tudor, his senior by fifteen years. This marriage gave him the title—the bare title—of King of England, but Charles V's heir had little leisure to enjoy this wholly formal crown. When his English wife died five years later they had had no children, and Philip had to yield to Mary's half-sister, Elizabeth.

He had to abandon his fond dream of encircling France, which had already been cherished by his father, and also the hope of uniting the sceptres of England and Spain in the hands of a Roman Catholic monarch. Philip's third wife, Elizabeth de Valois, a French princess, the daughter of Henri II and Catherine de' Medici, brought among her wedding presents the reconciliation between the Catholic King, her husband, and the Most Christian King, her father; her new subjects gave her the beautiful title of *Isabel de la Paz*, Isabella of the Peace. And yet, in 1572 Isabel de la Paz had been laid to rest under a black slab at the Escorial and Philip was already contemplating a fourth marriage.

But in the immediate future there was a more urgent task requiring the attention of His Catholic Majesty. Spain and Italy had been saved from the Protestant danger; the Mediterranean, from Tunis to Naples, including Corsica, Sardinia and Sicily, was free from the control of the infidel. But in the north, the Netherlands were threatened by Calvinist progress. Symbolically clad in rags, noblemen had gathered around William of Nassau, Prince of Orange, and had made an impressive protest against the coming of the Inquisition into their provinces. The Duke of Alva had been entrusted with the task of drowning this 'Beggars' Revolt' in blood.

William of Orange did not lay down his sword and France was now sending him help. As a matter of fact, most of the Huguenots who, under the Duke of Genlis, had come to help him, had been intercepted, crushed and killed by the

Spanish army before Mons. Nevertheless the situation in the Netherlands was compelling the King of Spain to watch the progress of Calvinism in France with unwavering attention, the more so because among the baggage of the noblemen killed in Mons had been found a letter from Charles IX, which proved collusion between the King of France and William of Orange. At the same time, and for the same reason, the French Catholics were looking to Philip of Spain.

Queen Elizabeth and her prisoner

If Geneva was the spiritual capital of the new faith, it was England which for over fifteen years—that is, since Queen Elizabeth's accession—had been its staunchest fortress. The destiny of the Protestant Queen was a strange one: in a way, she had been helped to the throne by the former so-called King of England, Philip II, champion of the Catholic faith. It is true that, in supporting Elizabeth, daughter of Henry VIII and Anne Boleyn, Philip's only thought was to oppose the claim of the other pretender, Mary Queen of Scots.

Yet Mary was Catholic and her claim to the English throne as sole legitimate descendant of the Tudors was upheld by learned doctors who relied on the decree according to which Elizabeth was branded a bastard. But those doctors were French, and the reason why Philip was helping Protestant Elizabeth against Catholic Mary was that the latter had just married Francis de Valois and had thus become Dauphine of France.

When ascending the throne after the death of her sister, who had earned the well-deserved nickname of Bloody Mary, Elizabeth had found her kingdom in a wretched state. In a concise style that was rare at that time, a council secretary summed up the situation as follows:

'The Queen poor, the realm exhausted, the nobility poor and powerless. Lack of good captains and soldiers. The people in complete disorder. Justice not executed. Everything too dear. Excess in meat, drink and apparel. Division among ourselves. War with France and Scotland. The French King bestriding the realm, having one foot in Calais and the other in Scotland. Steadfast enmity, but no steadfast friendship, abroad.'[1]

[1] Quoted by Sir Winston Churchill, *History of the English Speaking People*, Vol. II, p. 84.

That may have been true in 1558, but what was left of this sombre picture fourteen years later? The country was at peace with itself. England had become legally Protestant—neither Puritan nor Lutheran, but Anglican in a way which perfectly fitted the absolutism the Queen had inherited from her Tudor ancestors. Catholic agitation had subsided everywhere but in the North and in Scotland. Mary Stuart, who had sailed back to her kingdom after a brief reign in France with Francis II, had lost all authority and by her erratic life and successive marriages had drifted from scandal to murder and had barely managed to save her life by seeking refuge in Elizabeth's kingdom. Since 1568 the ex-Queen of Scots had been living under 'house arrest'. The Catholic noblemen in the northern counties who, a year later, had risen in the hope of freeing her, had been pitilessly crushed. Queen Elizabeth had triumphed within her kingdom.

At the same time she was about to triumph abroad, for although the Pope had excommunicated her in 1570, doubtless in order to 'legitimize' beforehand all that he was contemplating with Philip II, the French court was involved with her in matrimonial discussions, and Catherine de' Medici had proposed a marriage between the thirty-nine-year-old Queen and either the twenty-one-year-old heir to the throne, the Duke of Anjou, or even her youngest son, the Duke of Alençon, who was barely eighteen.

On Saint Peter's throne

In that summer of 1572 the Roman Catholic Church had a brand new Pope: Ugo Buoncompagni, St Peter's 225th successor, who had assumed the name of Gregory XIII at his election. He was a Bolognese and had lived a very gay life, even begetting a son, Giacomo. When ascending the throne of St Peter, one wonders whether he was already contemplating his reform of the Calendar which was to be the great accomplishment of his reign and to rescue his name from oblivion. It is possible, but it was more likely that the new Pope, scarcely three months after his election, was preoccupied with finding out the situation in which his immediate predecessors had left him. During the preceding twenty years no less than three Popes had ascended the Apostle's throne: Paul IV, Pius IV and Pius V.

Just at the moment when the Roman church suffered the attack of the Calvinists, the disastrous reign of Paul IV had done much to increase division within the Catholic fold and to distress conscientious Christians, while at the same time it provided the Reformers with even more powerful arguments, thanks to the Pope's corrupt administration and scandalous nepotism.

The people of Rome made no mistake about it, and the death of Paul IV was greeted by twelve days of violent rioting in the streets; the rebels—all of them good Catholics—had not only smashed the statue which Paul had erected to himself during his own lifetime, but they had also looted the Palace of the Inquisition.

The next Pope, Pius IV, in order to pacify the mob, had four of his predecessor's most obnoxious nephews tried and put to death. This hasty display of justice did not prevent him from bestowing the purple on his own nephew, Carlo Borromeo. This promotion, itself a piece of nepotism, was to become, because of Borromeo's outstanding personality, one of the most profitable deeds for the Church of Pius IV's reign. Borromeo, who at twenty-seven was an ascetic, succeeded in enforcing in Rome a strict reformation of the clergy's morale, while on a wider field he compelled the Council of Trent to resume and conclude its work after an interruption of eight years.

But Pius IV lacked any sense of militant activity and one of Carlo Borromeo's main achievements was to realize, as the main elector in the Conclave of 1566, that the Church needed above all a combatant Pope.

Pius V was this Pope, and he was almost the equal of the dangers which threatened the Church. Setting an example of austerity, looking for support to the Jesuits and the Oratory, he tried to galvanize the Christian world into action by reminding them of the permanence of the Turkish threat in the Mediterranean. One might say that in a sense he was 'the Pope of Lepanto'. It was said that shortly before his death he thought of undertaking an even more daring crusade with Philip II, which he would lead in person against the island fortress of Protestantism. Was he not preparing for it, moreover, when in 1570 he solemnly excommunicated Elizabeth of England?

Among the papers he bequeathed his successor there was at least one which was going to give endless worry to Gregory

XIII: it concerned the relations between the Roman Church and 'her eldest daughter', France, where Calvinism was progressing at such pace that no social class was immune.

From the stake to Court

That is exactly what the ultra-Catholic population of Paris was witnessing: they were exasperated and shocked. They took it as a mark of royal impotence, and some even said out loud, of royal complicity.

It is a fact that Protestantism had required only a few years to become a powerful political party, after having been just a form of personal belief at the time when the first martyrs had died at the stake. To understand how quickly things had developed, let us just remember how Protestants were dealt with at the end of Henri II's reign. The King had made up his mind to vanquish the opposition of some members of the Parliament of Paris, whose leader was Anne du Bourg; in Ecouen, a few days before the tourney in which he was to be killed, he signed an Edict, stating the line judges had to follow when dealing with heretics. There was just one kind of punishment: death at the stake, and the Edict was enforced from July 10, 1559, the day on which the King died. Thus in 1559 the only way by which the State dealt with the Huguenots was by fire.

Only thirteen years had passed since the Edict of Ecouen, and the Protestant party was counting princes of the blood among its members. Its influence on the nobility was increasing, while it was far from diminishing among the lower classes— with the exception of Paris. There were numerous Protestants among the King's councillors and those men were listened to and their advice often prevailed. It was even feared that France might finally break away from the Catholic Spain of Philip II and side openly with the 'Beggars' of the Netherlands.

At the same time, the Reformed Church, which had been accepted into the State, was maintaining its own troops, which were not the King's, and they were garrisoned in four powerful cities. To crown it all, the Most Christian King was giving his own sister, a daughter of France, a Valois Princess, in marriage to one of the Huguenot leaders. What had happened, during those thirteen years, to account for this stupendous progress?

The two Kings who had ascended the throne since Henri II's death, his sons Francis II and Charles IX, had had troubled reigns, and for the last ten years civil war had ceaselessly devastated the kingdom. Yet one has only to recall the main phases and vicissitudes of those Wars of Religion to realize that the Calvinists had never had the upper hand and were more often defeated than victorious. How could one bring an already passionately logical people to understand that such a situation had not halted the progress of the Protestant party?

Francis II had been a sickly boy, whose life was despaired of by the doctors almost at the time of his accession. During the few months of his reign, the Protestants had not yet been able to emerge from a semi-clandestine condition. The young king, physically and mentally unable to govern by himself, was under the influence of his young wife, Mary Stuart, and relinquished power into the hands of the Queen's uncles, the Guises, the powerful chiefs of the ultra-Catholic party. By handing over Anne du Bourg to the executioner, they had displayed their intention to carry out the stipulations of the Edict of Ecouen to the bitter end.

The increasing danger of the Protestant party had been revealed during Francis II's reign and the Guise dictatorship by the Amboise Conspiracy. The conspirators, among whom there was no important person, sought to kidnap the King and cut him off from the Guise influence. But the latter was warned in time and the plot miscarried. The subsequent repression was so atrocious and so widespread that the Catholics were entitled to hope that they were rid of any organized Protestant party for many years to come.

And yet, two years later, two armies met on a battlefield; one was led by the Guises, and the other was formed from those very Huguenots whose eradication had been too hastily proclaimed after Amboise.

But after December 1560 France had not merely a new King. Henri II's second son, when he was called to the throne after his brother's death, was just ten years old, and the Regency was assumed by his mother, Catherine de' Medici, who from that day on was the real ruler, actually if not legally, in spite of the fact that in 1563 she thought fit to have her son's majority declared.

Catherine, though a Catholic and the niece of a Pope, was forced from the start, by dismissing the Guises, to create a royalist third party between the two extreme groups, the

Catholics and the Protestants. With the help of the Chancellor Michel de l'Hôpital, she had even tried in vain to organize a courteous discussion between them, in the hope of bringing about a sort of religious unity, a sort of Gallicanism.

Faithful—maybe by mere coincidence—to the foreign policies of Francis I, who had allied himself both to the Lutheran princes and to Soliman the Magnificent, she refused to side wholly with Philip II, as the Catholic party wanted her to do, without wishing to associate too openly with Protestant England or the Netherland rebels. This double neutral policy at home and abroad, was full of danger: it could not fail to incite the two antagonistic groups to a trial of force, if only to compel the royal government to side with the victorious party. The Catholics had probably realized that the idea of the Amboise conspiracy was a sound one and they decided to kidnap the King, but to take greater care than their adversaries had done. On the other hand, the Protestants, warned of this plan by the Queen Mother, and incensed by the slaughter of sixty of their brothers, murdered in cold blood by the Guises while they were attending a service at Wassy, took up arms.

War went on for a whole year, from March 1562 to March 1563. Both sides appealed to foreign powers for help; the Catholics were more faithful to the *Triumvirs*—Guise, Montmorency and St André—than to the King, and they appealed to the Pope and to Philip II; the Protestants, under Condé, enlisted German mercenaries and signed a treaty with Elizabeth, ceding Le Havre in return for instant help.

From beginning to end, the campaign, traditionally known as the First War of Religion, turned in favour of the Catholics. They were not only successful in their own version of the Amboise Conspiracy, taking the King and his family 'under their protection', but they victoriously demonstrated their superiority on every battlefield, Rouen and Dreux especially. Nothing less than the murder at Orleans of their leader, Francis de Guise, could compel them to accept the peace offered by Catherine. It did not take their victories into sufficient account, and they merely accepted it as a truce enabling them to rest awhile and reorganize.

On the other hand, the Huguenots were not very pleased with this 'patched-up peace', since the liberty of worship granted only to the nobility was likely to prevent making converts at the lower level. Calvin realized it at once and called Condé, who had signed it, a 'wretch'.

It was not long before war broke out again, and the Protestants were again badly defeated. They failed in a new attempt to kidnap the King at Meaux and lost the battles of Jarnac and Moncontour. All they could do was to save their army at the last moment from total destruction and more or less retrieve the situation on the Loire, thanks to a clever manoeuvre by Admiral de Coligny. That sufficed to enable them to negotiate a new peace on an honourable basis. The Peace of St Germain, signed in 1570, was not only honourable, but definitely favourable to the Protestants. It gave them four 'places of security' and the right to be invested with the principal State offices, and it opened the King's Council to Coligny, who played a leading part in it, not to mention the fact that one of its main results was the engagement of the Catholic princess Marguerite de Valois to the Huguenot leader Henri de Bourbon, King of Navarre, son of Antoine de Bourbon, a nonentity, and Jeanne d'Albret, a passionate and devout woman.

In short, no striking achievement, and certainly not the military results of the first two Wars of Religion, could account for the political good fortune of the Protestant party. And it is no less certain that this good fortune—witness the festivities being prepared for the wedding of Marguerite and the King of Navarre, and the arrival in Paris in full array of the whole of the Protestant nobility—helped to put Paris in an evil mood.

It is difficult to accept the notion that anything is accountable in politics or in history, the more so when it proves to be unsatisfactory and when events yield no explanation: one may have to try and probe the minds and hearts of the main characters of the drama. One must confess that some of them were above, or below, average level.

Queen and Mother

First of all, let us take Catherine de' Medici. In August 1572 the Queen Mother was just fifty-three. She was not, and had never been, a beauty, even when she was fourteen and Angiolo Bronzino had painted the *duchessina*'s portrait, trying to be both faithful and flattering at once, as she was about to be married to Francis I's youngest son. She was now a stout, active, fidgetty woman, whose black garments made her complexion look even more swarthy. She had heavy eyebrows, big protruding eyes, a large nose and a heavy underlip. Yet everybody—friend, courtier or enemy—recognised her impressive bearing, her authority, and above all, her unquestionable intelligence. According to Giovanni Michieli, the Venetian Ambassador in Paris, she was behaving, 'not as a woman, but as a man of great courage, well versed in the art of governing kingdoms'. This 'man of courage' who was Catherine was in full power. Michieli had already noticed it in 1560; he wrote: 'In the Government, the Queen Mother is acknowledged as the one whose will is supreme . . . and in the Council there is no leader but she.'

So who was this all-powerful Queen Mother and which influence had worked upon her mind to endow her with the intellect of a first-rate statesman? In tracing her origins, one usually limits oneself to her father's ancestors. She was a Medici through him, and Lorenzo the Magnificent's granddaughter. The latter was the Prince to whom Machiavelli had inscribed his famous book. Catherine was more than Italian: she was a sixteenth-century Florentine and for Frenchmen she embodied all the vices and some of the questionable qualities of her compatriots and contemporaries: realism, freedom from scruples, trickery and dissimulation, and cruelty, or anyway, lack of sensitiveness, so that one might be tempted to explain the whole of her personality by her Italian ancestry and the teachings of Machiavelli. But one must not forget that through her mother, Madeleine de la Tour d'Auvergne, she may have inherited some of the defects and virtues of the people of Auvergne. Also, it would be wrong to forget Catherine's own past, which did more than heredity to forge her character.

From infancy until the day she set herself up as regent—that is, for more than forty years—she got nothing out of life but bitterness and frustration. She lost both her parents when she was scarcely ten days old and she spent the first years of her life in the restless, faction-torn atmosphere of Florence. Deprived of her own duchy of Urbino by her own guardian and cousin, Pope Clement VII, she spent several months as a prisoner of the extremists who had seized power over the city of the Red Lily. It was merely the fact that she was a convenient hostage that saved her life or prevented her from being sent to a brothel, as was suggested by the most excited of the Arrabbiati! Her marriage to the son of Francis I, who seemed to have the least chance of reigning, had been nothing but an episode in the matrimonial policy of the Pope, her guardian. Her life at the French court as a Princess, then as Dauphine, and then as Queen, did not bring her happiness either.

Catherine never forgot anything, neither the horror of civil war, nor the anguish which gnawed at her during the first ten years of her married life, as she was thought to be barren and she dreaded to be repudiated, nor her constant humiliation as wife and queen by the flaunted liaison between Henri II and Diane de Poitiers.

When at last, through drugs, astrology and sorcery, her barrenness was overcome and she was pregnant ten times within twelve years, she suffered further terrors and humiliations. For the Medici blood was tainted, even more than that of the Valois, and Catherine was made the more aware of it since almost all her children were abnormal, sickly or suffering from the King's evil, while the Chevalier d'Angoulême, her husband's natural son by the beautiful Scot, Jane Fleming, was a strong and healthy lad.

More frustration came to her after Henri's death, as the new king's young wife, Mary Stuart, already Queen of Scotland, with all the pride of her sixteen years and her ancestry, flaunted her contempt for the 'Florentine shopkeeper'. Thus for over forty years Catherine de' Medici had had to swallow insults in words or deeds, while pretending not to notice them. It had been a strange school of dissimilation, which, even more than her origins, serves to explain the peculiarities of her political behaviour, without taking into account the accumulated rancour, the bottled-up hatred which were bound to weigh upon the Florentine shopkeeper's acts of government. Take for example her attitude towards the Guises, whom she had never forgiven for having sided with Mary Stuart, their niece, to keep her apart from the King throughout Francis II's reign.

Catherine's personality is less enigmatic when considered in the light of her origins and experience of life, and the apparent contradictions in her line of policy seem less puzzling. A granddaughter on the model of the Prince, she took to heart the essentials of the political realism which gave such originality to Machiavelli's thought. She wholly believed that 'things of consequence happen to Princes who set little value by their word': she willingly agreed that 'one must be loved and feared, but it is difficult, and if one has to make a choice it is better to be feared'. Above all, she took as her motto the following statement: 'A Prince's job is to keep his realm, and every possible means he uses to do it will always be deemed honest and he will be praised by everybody.' Consequently, she made up her mind to use 'every possible means', either the potent charms of her maids of honour—who were uncommonly lovely girls— or the services of some hired murderer.

The daughter of a princess of Auvergne, as soon as she was in power she summoned to Court an obscure judge from Riom whom she entrusted with the task of carrying out her policy. She was on better terms with her Auvergne countryman, Michel de l'Hôpital, than with any other minister. Haunted by the memory of the dark hours in Florence, she put peace at home above religion: though the niece and disciple of several Popes, she never ceased to seek a precarious, but peaceful coexistence even after the failure of the Colloquy of Poissy, with the result that she was as roundly abused in Rome as in Geneva.

Rome never forgot a letter in which she had suggested that the Pope should limit religion to the Ten Commandments in order to stop argument between Christians. On the other hand, it is unlikely that the Pastors of the Consistory of Geneva ever knew that, when Catherine heard a report that the Huguenots were victorious at Dreux, she merely remarked: 'Well, we shall then pray to God in French.'[1] From those many years of humiliation and humility at the French court she had retained one main concern: to be the undisputed ruler of the kingdom and to settle all her children on various European thrones. Hence her marriage policy, which was going to involve her in more trouble: Elizabeth married Philip II of Spain, Charles IX was connected by marriage with Maximilian of Austria, Marguerite married Henri of Navarre, while Henri d'Anjou and Francis d'Alençon were offered with unseemly insistence to Elizabeth of England.

While Catherine as Regent wielded undisputed power in the name of Charles IX, she probably lived the finest years of her life. Rebellions and all the problems which cropped up, far from repelling her, acted as an incentive and made her relish more deeply and fully her own cunning and talents.

[1] Voltaire, note to *La Henriade* (II, 17).

The Queen Mother was not allowed to bask for long in these unadulterated satisfactions. The Florentine astrologer who had cast the *duchessina*'s horoscope shortly after her birth had foretold a life 'full of sorrow, trouble and storms'. Catherine was quite willing to undergo them all for her children's sake, and for her sons above all, but they were themselves going to be the very cause of it. Within a short time, an ever increasing silent hatred grew up between Charles IX and Anjou, the Queen's favourite child. Her very love for him led the King to look outside the family circle for support against them both. In 1572 Charles IX had found someone on whom to lean in order to escape his mother's tutelage and to make her pay for the exclusive love she showed for the Duc d'Anjou. Coligny's sudden influence over the King can be explained in no other way, nor can the consuming Italian hatred the Queen Mother felt for him.

The King, God's death!

What kind of man was this young king who was just beginning to show a will of his own, after having been for twelve years on the throne and of age for eight? Seen from a distance, when laughing and joking with his usual playmates, it was difficult to believe that he was already twenty-two: he had the figure of a sickly adolescent, too thin for his size, hollow-chested and with drooping shoulders. At close range this first impression vanished, giving way to a completely different one: he had the refined, haggard look of a man prematurely worn out, whose real age could not be ascertained; his sallow complexion and bilious eyes betrayed liver trouble; he had a bitter twist at the corners of his mouth and feverish eyes. Another contrast was in store for those who heard him speak: this sickly-looking youth, whose weakness was so obvious, had the broad, coarse style of speaking of a stable-lad, every sentence being puctuated by a resounding oath. All these contradictory signs revealed his physical defects and his neuropathic psychism. For Charles IX was first and foremost a sick man. The tuberculosis which consumed him had transformed the charming, pleasant and lovable boy, who had been adored by his subjects during a long tour of his realm, first into an irritable youth, then an irritable man, quick-tempered and capable, like all weak people, of the worst forms of violence; and the more sick he grew, the worse became the vices born of his illness.

His passion for hunting, riding and violent exercise, his interest in forging weapons, his wild bouts of eating and drinking, and his ruffianly blasphemy arose from the fact that he felt himself sinking physically. But the life he led and the excesses in which he indulged could only aggravate his condition and intensify his complexes. With unconscious cruelty, Catherine had furthered the trouble by showing only too well how much she preferred Henri d'Anjou, the second of her three surviving sons.

Charles felt, and certainly knew, that he could not live long and would die without legitimate heirs, and he could hardly bear to be attended always by his younger brother, better looking, more robust and in better health than himself, who would ascend the throne after his death. To make things worse, this well-hated brother had chosen to be a soldier, in which profession their father had shone, but Charles (to his own fury) was unable to follow. Catherine, proud of her younger son and wishing to make a popular hero of him, did all she could to enable him to indulge his taste for military display. When Anne de Montmorency died, she wished to have him appointed Constable of France, and only the King's flat refusal—his first attempt at showing a will of his own—brought the plan to naught. The office of Constable was therefore still vacant, but Anjou, appointed lieutenant-general, had reaped laurels on the battlefields of Jarnac and Moncontour, while Charles had no other way to vent his feelings than to hunt for hours to the very end of his constantly dwindling strength. He hunted in order to kill, for he soon acquired a taste for blood, and almost every day he needed the bitter sensation, the uneasy satisfaction of seeing the pulsating entrails and the hounds on the quarry.

Yet this King who was so close to madness, this sick man on the brink of frenzy, this son and brother devoured by jealousy and hatred, still kept in some deep recess of his heart a place for purer feelings, more in conformity to those of earlier years.

He was still a 'gentle companion' for the privileged few who shared his pleasures. Among them were several famous Huguenots: La Rochefoucauld, whom the King addressed as 'Foucauld', for short, and was the last each evening to bid the King good night. There was also Téligny, the charming but credulous Protestant diplomat, who had lately become Admiral de Coligny's son-in-law. It was to Téligny that Charles IX said once, unburdening his mind about the councillors whom Catherine had selected for him: 'Téligny, do you want me to speak freely? I don't trust any of those people. Tavannes' ambition is suspect; Vieilleville is interested in nothing but good wine; Cossé is too avaricious; Montmorency cares for nothing but hunting and falconry; the Comte de Retz is a Spaniard; the other lords at court and those of my council are fools; to tell you the whole truth, my secretaries of State are unfaithful to me, and so, as a matter of fact, I don't know where to begin.'[1]

When he was with his few friends, the King sometimes could show himself as a good musician, whose pure and tuneful voice was often praised, or as a charming poet, the pupil of Amyot, who had once written to Ronsard:

> '*Tous deux également nous portons des couronnes,*
> *Mais, roi, je les reçois, poète, tu les donnes.*'[2]

It was also as a poet, or, better, as a sick child and unhappy youth that he had been known by two women, both of them of modest origin and both of them Huguenots; in their arms he tried to find peace and solace and to forget his too heavy crown. One was his nurse, the other Marie Touchet. The sweet, lovely Marie Touchet had been his mistress for over six years. He had met her on his way back from his long tour of France, when Catherine had shown the young King his realm, and it had been love at first sight.

In Orleans the King insisted on visiting a small apothecary, Jean Touchet, out of friendship for and gratitude to the court Doctor, Mathy, who was Touchet's father-in-law. The apothecary had a daughter whose beauty had overwhelmed the King. Marie was just fifteen and she fell in love at once with the prince charming who was barely a year older. She did so without false modesty or calculation; she just fell in love. In 1572 Charles and Marie were still as deeply in love as on the first day, and the King's marriage in 1570 to Elisabeth of Austria, a very attractive princess, whose only wish was to make her husband care for her, had not affected the King's passion for Marie. She felt so sure of herself and of her lover that she said with a smile to

---

[1] Pierre de l'Estoile, *Mémoires pour servir à l'histoire de France.*

[2] 'Both of us wear crowns, but I receive them as a King, while you impart them as a poet.'

those who told her of the marriage: 'Oh, I am not afraid of that German girl!' Retiring and completely disinterested, Marie lived always in the King's shadow. Charles was still writing verse for her. One of the many sonnets he inscribed to her began:

'Toucher, aimer, est ma devise.'[1]

Thus there were a few friends and two women who found something lovable in Charles IX. After the Peace of St Germain, when the Huguenots came back to Court, the King showed Coligny a respectful affection and a far too ostentatious, though sincere, trust in him. Feeling weak, helpless, sick and frustrated in his filial love, Charles badly needed the support of an older person in whom he could find an adviser, and he had been at once struck by Coligny's masterful personality. The Admiral's royalist loyalty reassured him. His statesmanship impressed him and Coligny's ambitious intelligence had done the rest.

Above everything else, Charles IX wanted to be a great king, and Coligny was bringing him prestige through the great overseas expeditions which he was promoting as Admiral of France. A far-away shore where a few emigrants—even though they were Huguenots—had hoisted the flag that bore the lilies of France, had already been named Carolina after the King. The campaigns which Coligny was urging in Europe also fitted in very well with the King's wishes. There was glory to reap in them, with the added satisfaction of worrying Philip II, of whose power and fame, after Lepanto, he was jealous. Consequently, Charles was more and more willing openly to side with Coligny against the Queen Mother and the Council and help the 'Beggars' of the Netherlands.

The King was always yielding to some influence and always likely to change his mind at a moment's notice, and at that time he was completely under the Admiral's sway. He was ready to accept without question whatever Coligny proposed. He addressed him as 'Father', not without a certain provocative satisfaction. In this way he brought as much enthusiasm to forcing the Navarre marriage upon his sister as to approving the raising of troops to fight in Flanders.

It is not surprising that, in the eyes of Paris and the Catholics,

[1] 'To touch and to live is my motto'. There is a pun in the word *toucher* (Touchet).

Charles seemed to be dominated by the Huguenots, among whom he had chosen his friends, his mistress and his adviser. Nor was it surprising that Catherine, who had done much to bring the Protestants back into the State, had suddenly panicked at seeing herself about to be superseded by the Admiral, who seemed about to become a sort of Mayor of the Palace. Of course, the Queen Mother never hesitated to change her line of policy. According to Machiavelli, 'any means' were convenient under such circumstances. Things had come to such a state that she was now ready to use the means she had tried to avoid so far, knowing how dangerous it was: make use of the Catholic party with Guise as leader.

Revenge

Each time the name of Guise was mentioned, the heart of Paris beat quicker. Paris delighted in those men who were fine horsemen: more handsome than intelligent, with more courage than brains, and so narrow-minded that they never conceived any scruple about anything. They were a godsend to a city in which, at that time, nothing was more hateful than toleration.

The Guises, whose height, tremendous physical toughness and abundant health were in striking contrast to the sickly weakness of the last Valois, came from a great and ancient family, which meant a great deal at that time. They belonged to the family of the Dukes of Lorraine, descending slightly more directly from St Louis than the Valois themselves. Among their distant ancestors the Lorraines also had a direct descendant of Charlemagne, a fact which enabled them to question the rights of the Capetians to the French crown.

In 1572, the third duke, Henri, was a youth of twenty-two—the same age as the King. He had inherited his title some ten years earlier and had waged war against the Turks and the Huguenots, thus defending the Faith, so to speak. Yet he had not been able to forget that his father, the Duke Francis, was always referred to—far too frequently—as the 'Great M de Guise'.

It is a fact that Francis, the first Guise prince to be nick-named Scarface (Le Balafré), was an outstanding personality. His military gifts were great and he was one of the first captains of his time, inflicting on Charles V at Metz his first defeat. On the other hand, he was responsible for the outbreak of the First

War of Religion: for at Wassy, on Sunday, March 1, 1562, it was Francis de Guise who ordered his men to massacre the Protestants who had gathered in a barn to attend divine service. At the point of death, Francis de Guise confessed: 'The inconvenience inflicted on the people of Wassy took place against my will, as I had no intention to do them any harm.' Nevertheless there were a hundred victims of this 'inconvenience', including twenty-three dead, both men and women, and it was followed by wars and disturbances which in 1572 had lasted ten years and seemed only temporarily at an end.

Finally, and above all, Francis de Guise played a leading part even after his death, because of the very circumstances in which it occurred. On February 18, 1563, while his troops were besieging Orleans, he was riding back to camp in the evening, attended by three officers, when he was shot by a Huguenot, Poltrot de Méré, who had been waiting for him. The shots were fired almost at point blank. Scarface died six days later, begging that his enemies 'should be forgiven the insult they had done him by killing him'; but at the same time he named his enemies, beginning with Admiral Coligny. Of the murdered Duke's last speech, his widow, Anne d'Este, and his son Henri only remembered the conclusion, his accusation of Coligny, forgetting the pardon 'ordered' by François.

Admittedly, the Admiral's attitude was not likely to soothe infuriated people, and the least that can be said is that he cared more for truth than for tact. In a letter to the Queen, which was immediately published and widely publicised by the Huguenots, he courageously demanded to be confronted with Poltrot de Méré. At the same time, he did not seek to deny that he had seen the murderer shortly before the crime, and that he had paid him to spy upon the Duke de Guise. He added that 'when the said Poltrot told him that it would be easy to dispatch the Duke de Guise, he had said nothing about whether that would be a good or a bad thing'.

As soon as Francis de Guise had been buried with regal pomp, and Poltrot de Méré pulled to pieces by four horses in such a way that Léonore d'Humières, Guillaume de Montmorency's wife, 'fainted at the sight and died almost at once', the Guise family in deep mourning threw themselves at the little king's feet, demanding justice against Coligny. Catherine had other things to worry about, and she was not sorry to be rid of such a

1   GASPARD DE COLIGNY

Contemporary drawing. School of Clouet
(*Bibliotheque Ste Genevieve*)

2   TWO SCENES FROM THE WARS OF RELIGION

    a   Siege of Chartres by the Prince de Condé, 1568 (G = M de Piles; H = d'Andelot)

    b   Battle of Jarnac, 1569 (A = Coligny and d'Andelot; C = Montgomery; D = Briquemault; H = La Rochefoucauld)   *Bib. Nat.*

tiresome man. Without much ceremony she hastily dismissed those haughty Guises who had always been so full of contempt for her, the 'Florentine shopkeeper'. Shortly afterwards, she had a judgment delivered, discharging Coligny of all complicity. From that time on, the Lorraine princes gave only second thoughts to patriotism, loyalty and even religion. The one thing that mattered was the revenge they had been denied.

As his brother was dead and his nephew but a child, the Cardinal of Lorraine assumed the direction of the ultra-Catholic party. He who had been a terrible 'debater' at the Colloquy of Poissy and was always advised by the Jesuit, Edmond Auger, had practically made an act of allegiance to Philip II. In November 1568 he wrote to him: 'There is no family in this kingdom more prompt and more dedicated to Your Majesty's service than ours.' After the privileges granted to the Protestants at St Germain, he was more intent than ever to see Philip II enforce order in the kingdom of France.

For her part, the widow of the murdered Duke, beautiful Anne d'Este, of whom Ronsard had written that 'Cupid himself used to live in her looks', she did not mourn long: she soon married another Lorraine prince, the Duke de Nemours. But, true to her Italian blood, she had not renounced her sacred oath of vengeance, taken before the corpse of Scarface. As to the young Duke, not satisfied with seeking to punish the man whom his father had named as his real murderer—and there may be reason for it—he also had a personal reason to seek to punish the Huguenots in general and Coligny in particular, the King's 'evil genius'. In August 1572 the young prince had been thwarted in love and his self-esteem had been deeply wounded when he had had to give place to Henri de Navarre and renounce the lovely Princess Marguerite, who was his mistress and whom he hoped to make his wife. When the King had heard of their affaire, his anger had been so great that Henri de Guise, to save his life, had been compelled at dead of night to send for Catherine of Cleves, a young widow who was passionately intent on finding a second husband, and marry her there and then in the private chapel of the Nemours mansion, so that he could present her to the King the next morning as the Duchesse de Guise. One must agree that it was enough to put any proud, vindictive prince in a bad temper. And, as was usual among the Guises after the murder of François, one man was held responsible for anything unpleasant that happened: Coligny.

My father, the Admiral

Consequently, it seems that in August 1572 one man enjoyed the unpleasant privilege of gathering to himself, for very diverse reasons, the most widespread hatred; Gaspard de Coligny, Seigneur de Chatillon, Grand Admiral of France.

He had been for many years the undisputed leader of the Protestant party and he was just fifty-three: exactly the same age as the Queen Mother. Nevertheless, he was the traditionally patriarchal figure, probably on account of his stern and emaciated face, his already grey beard, the impression of gravity and melancholy that issued from his whole being, and his well-known austerity. One would have thought that he was a pastor rather than a warrior, yet Coligny had been a soldier first and foremost, although, despite his title, he had never fought on the King's ships. This admiral was a landlubber, an outstanding infantry tactician.

Sixteenth century people saw nothing incongruous in that, for one could be a great admiral without having set foot on any ship but a barge in order to cross the Seine; one could also be a Master of Horse and a poor horseman, the prior of an abbey while leading the gayest of lives, and even—as was the case with one of Coligny's brothers—a cardinal, a Huguenot and a married man all at the same time.[1]

Gaspard de Coligny had been knighted on the battlefield of Cerisoles and, after the capture of Carignano in 1544, Henri II had appointed him Colonel-General of the French infantry. He had discharged his command with the industry he put into everything, so that Sainte-Marthe wrote of him that 'he organized the infantry and made regulations which are still in use today'.[2] In 1552 he had been appointed Admiral of France by Henri II. In that authority he had endeavoured to send the Royal flag as far as possible, to the shores of Brazil and Florida, to the annoyance of Philip of Spain, who was irritated to see 'the French perched so near his own conquests'.

Coligny was converted to Calvinism in 1556 and at first it was only with the greatest caution, and thanks to the protection

---

[1] Odet de Coligny had never received holy orders.
[2] Sainte-Marthe, *Traité historique des Armes de France et de Navarre*, 1673.

of his uncle, the Constable of Montmorency, that he was able to escape Henri II's persecution and disfavour. Later, when trouble began again, the Admiral openly stepped into the religious and political struggle, and, strange as it seems, was induced to do so by the Queen Mother, who took him for a moderate, useful member of his party, who might succeed in creating a third and intermediary group, while she was endeavouring to do the same on the Catholic side. And it was the Queen who brought Coligny back to court in 1571; she was so pleased with what she had achieved that she wrote, without concealing her pleasure: 'At last, we have the Admiral here, in Blois.'

Coligny's presence at court implied the acceptance by the Protestants of the Queen Mother's policy, and their willingness to live under the Edict of Pacification which sanctioned the Peace of St Germain. The Queen knew well that Coligny was no disciple of Machiavelli, but she did not understand his real personality. His ambition did not derive from greed or from a craving for honours, but it was none the less real. As a party leader, the Admiral was not content with a half-victory, even if it had been the unhoped-for outcome of a defeat. As Catherine was offering him the means to influence the King, and to influence French politics, Coligny seized this unexpected opportunity. During the next month the Court saw Coligny's star rise; Charles IX was seen to closet himself with the Admiral for hours on end, and the King had been heard to address him as 'Father'. More than that, courtiers noticed with dismay that, when he was with the Admiral, the King refrained from swearing, for fear of shocking the strict Protestant who had become his chief adviser.

The Catholic party, the Queen Mother, the Guises and the whole of Paris had observed the results of the King's sudden fancy, and the foreign Ambassadors in Paris sent reports to Philip II, the Pope and the Republic of Venice, that the Most Christian King had adopted as his favourite councillor the leader of the heretics, from whose disastrous influence one might expect dire results. In spite of the defeat at Mons of the French troops sent to help the Princes of Orange, an alliance might bind France to Queen Elizabeth, the Lutheran princes, the Netherlands rebels and even the Sultan, in order to make war against His Catholic Majesty.

The marriage of Henri de Navarre and Marguerite de Valois, which was solemnized in Paris even before the papal dispensation had arrived, according to a form of service which permitted the bridegroom not to be present at mass, added scandal to anxiety. A story was widely spread that at the King's last council, Coligny, who advocated war in the Netherlands, had violently quarrelled with Marshal de Tavannes speaking for the Catholic majority, and even the word 'treason' was used! Having vainly used all his arguments, Coligny had added, staring fixedly at Catherine: 'The King refuses to make war. May it please God that another one won't be forced on him which will not be so easy to renounce.'

The real meaning of that sentence has often been discussed. Was it a threat or not? Coligny was not the man to say 'May it please God' in order to express desire for an assent. It is easy to see that he meant: 'I hope that I am mistaken but . . .' Yet Catherine and her councillors chose to see a threat in it. It was repeated and distorted, so that it gave the Paris mob a new reason to hate the Admiral and the Huguenots.

What about Paris?

Let us conclude here this rough sketch of the leading characters in a tragedy which, in August 1572, seemed about to begin. There was no longer any doubt: the chain of events during the ten years since the outbreak of the First War of Religion, and the developments of the home and foreign situation following the unsatisfactory Peace of St Germain in 1570, were leading irresistibly, in a dramatic crescendo, to a major tragedy.

Every drama requires a setting and sometimes a large chorus. One might have thought that Paris and its mob would have been content to play that passive, or semi-active part: it was not. The first city in the kingdom had never agreed to play a minor part when something happened and never will.

The people of Paris had a reputation to maintain: they had always made a choice, whether good or bad. In the past, they had courageously fought against the Normans and welcomed the English as liberators; they had compelled the Dauphin Charles to wear Etienne Marcel's red and blue hood,[1] and taken part in the Cabochiens' ferocious rebellion.[2] Paris had never

[1] In 1356.
[2] *c.* 1412

36

been able to remain neutral and indifferent while political adversaries were at each other's throats. This was going to happen again, and the capital's preferences were already known.

Paris once more was aiming at being the setting, as well as the leading actor, of the drama. No Parisian of 1572 would have been surprised when reading the following appreciations of the part he played, written several centuries later: 'In the absence of men big enough for such a cause, Paris itself was the leader of the Catholic party in France in the sixteenth century.'[1]

With its 210,000 inhabitants and 12,000 houses on either side of the river, Paris was still kept within very narrow boundaries. To the north, the gates of Montmartre, St Denis, St Martin and of the Temple, all along the ramparts, gave access to bad roads which led to far-away villages such as Ménilmontant, Villeneuve-les-Gravois or Montfaucon.

One went sometimes to Montfaucon[2] to look at the gallows. Their sixteen stone pillars rose more than thirty feet from a platform of masonry, itself eighteen feet high, and from the top of this sinister colonnade fifty or sixty decomposed or dried corpses swayed in the wind in rusty, creaking chains.

To the east, the impressive pile of the Bastille, standing as the limit of the city, reminded passers-by of the King's power.

To the west, the city was beginning to break through the tight stone corset which had been fastened round her by Philippe-Auguste, to make her more secure: the Queen Mother had entrusted Philibert Delorme and Jean Bullant with the task of erecting a new palace for her in the Tuileries. It was now completed and within its walls were marvels known to the people only by hearsay: an aviary, a pond, a menagerie, an orangery, a warren. But the new ramparts, from the Tuileries to the Seine, made little progress, so that the old gates still stood between the Louvre and the Tuileries.

Finally, to the south, on the left bank of the river, the city had extended even less. It did not go beyond the gates of St Jacques, St Michel, St Victor, or the Génovéfains gardens. That district, with the Sorbonne at its centre, surrounded by numerous colleges, was the almost exclusive domain of rowdy students, whom honest citizens avoided. In fact, battles raged

---

[1] Vicomte de Vaux, *La lutte religieuse en France au XVI siècle.*
[2] The gallows were situated in an area bounded now by the St Martin canal, the Rues des Ecluses St Martin, Grange-aux-Belles and Louis Blanc.

between one college and another on the most trifling pretext. Usually those feuds ended in hearty reconciliations, and former foes in one vast crowd swept out beyond the ramparts to the Pré-aux-Clercs to invade and ransack houses and gardens, or tear down the railings and strip the orchards of the Abbey of St Germain-des-Prés.[1] On the far side of the Gate of Buci, the Faubourg St Germain, which had been razed during the Hundred Years War and had gone back to waste land, was now largely rebuilt and beginning to attract a few noble families.

However, the principal activities in Paris were grouped on the right bank, with the Court at the Louvre and the nobility in the Marais, while in between, burghers, merchants and artisans shared the streets round the Town Hall and the Halles.

Lawyers still had their headquarters on the island of the *Cité*, the one connecting link between the two banks, apart from ferries, barges and boats plying their ways backwards and forward. Paris at that time had only five bridges, very close to one another. Three connected the right bank to the *Cité*: the Pont-aux-Meuniers, the Pont-au-Change and the Pont Notre-Dame. Two led from the *Cité* to the left bank, the Pont St Michel and the Petit Pont. As for the banks of the Seine, in spite of some work carried out under Henri II, they hardly deserved to be described as *quais*. A fairly large number of boats were there for crossing the river to the islands or to the far bank, and especially for transporting, loading and unloading the merchandise brought along on the river.

The ever-increasing traffic did not confine itself to the harbours of Paris. The whole city, compressed with constant difficulty within its medieval boundaries, was in constant agitation from sunrise to sunset. The narrow, dirty, badly paved streets never found any semblance of quiet and silence except at night when the police patrolled them.

[1] The reader's attention should be drawn to the fact that there were—and still are—two districts in Paris known as St Germain. On the right bank of the Seine stood the church of *St Germain l'Auxerrois*, next door to the Louvre, inside the city walls; on the left bank was the large Abbey of *St Germain des Prés*, beyond the walls. Both places will be mentioned quite often in the following chapters. St Germain l'Auxerrois and part of the Rue des Fossés St Germain still exist, though the district has been almost completely rebuilt. The church of St Germain des Prés and parts of the monastery still stand on the Boulevard St Germain. Gothic parts of the abbey—a large hall and a staircase—have lately been discovered in a house in Rue de l'Abbaye nearby.

Paris was far from being a law-abiding city: it harboured some six to seven thousand thieves, and eight to nine thousand beggars and tramps. Consequently, the Provost of the Merchants, who was the President of the City Council, assisted by four aldermen, the King's attorney, his secretary and his tax-collector, to whom had just been added twenty-six councillors and ten sergeants, was at the head of fairly large armed forces. Counting the city militia, with officers commanding detachments of fifty, forty or ten men, three companies of arquebusiers, bowmen and archers, and the Royal or city watchmen, there were altogether several thousand people legally entitled to bear arms.

Of course, they did not always use them to protect the city against an invader, or the inhabitants against outrages committed by rowdies, Corsican or Italian bandits, French mischiefmakers and various other kinds of unsavoury gaol-birds. More than once, the city guards had taken arms, more or less spontaneously, to attack the heretics. For instance, they looted Huguenot churches in the Rues Mouffetard and Popincourt, an achievement which earned the Constable de Montmorency the nickname Captain Burn-Benches; again, after Wassy, Paris took arms to give a triumphant welcome to François de Guise; and more recently, when Coligny ordered the cross of Gastines[1] to be taken to the Cemetery of the Innocents,[2] as it commemorated in the very centre of Paris the execution of Huguenots who had been caught holding secret services, the citizens had again taken up arms and displayed their bad temper by rioting, looting and burning houses, and murdering.

It was known that this discontent was growing. Preachers were turning the Paris churches virtually into political clubs and they had no difficulty in encouraging this. From their pulpits they rained abuse and threats on those whose leniency to the Huguenots they regarded as treason. Charles IX was nicknamed Ahab, his mother Jezebel, and as for Coligny, the mob was reminded that he had delivered Le Havre to England, opened the frontiers to Jean Casimir's German soldiers and that he had twice besieged Paris and reduced its inhabitants to starvation. The King was now most friendly with him, and yet Coligny

[1] The cross, erected on the spot where stood the house of the Gastines, which was pulled down by an order of Parliament, was at the north-west corner of the crossroad where the Rue St Denis meets the Rue des Lombards.

[2] The spot where the Cemetery of the Innocents stood is now the Place des Innocents.

had been sentenced to death by Parliament less than three years earlier as a rebel and a traitor. He had been hanged in effigy and his coat of arms had been broken and disgraced. More than that, there was an edict offering 10,000 gold crowns as reward to any person of any social standing who would seize, arrest and bring the Admiral to justice alive, and 2,000 crowns if he was killed outright. The Admiral had had a hairbreadth escape when M. de Maurevert, who was in consequence nicknamed the *King's killer*, shot at him and barely missed him: he had confused Coligny with one of his attendants and had shot and killed M. de Mouy, who was walking beside him. Yet Maurevert's 'services' had been well rewarded by the King, who was content to take the intention alone into consideration and give him the collar of the Order of St Michel!

That was quite enough to provide pithy subjects for any number of sermons to inflame the people of Paris. Other fuel was added to the fire: those who, either clerics or laymen, high or low, had planned or permitted the marriage of Marguerite de Valois to a Protestant, had committed mortal sin; the disquieting gathering in Paris for that wedding of hundreds of Protestant noblemen from the provinces; the fact that they had brought their richest apparel, valuable jewels and coffers full of gold in order to look their best at court; then a few more remarks to show the Huguenots and their accomplices as the party of the Protestant war, together with the vanquished soldiers of Mons, against the Catholic King, the victor of Lepanto. . . . By such sermons Paris was turned into a barrel of gunpowder ready to explode with the tiniest spark.

Away with the Admiral!

The spark was to be deliberately fired by Catherine: it sprang from an arquebuse on August 22nd, at about eleven in the morning.

Not that the Queen Mother herself had waited patiently with her finger on the trigger for the Admiral to pass within range: these were the duties of servants, to which a great lady did not lower herself.

But to plan a political assassination down to its most minute details and to its most distant consequences, to choose carefully the men who would carry it out, and above all, so to arrange things that others would shoulder the responsibility and suffer the consequences—these were what a queen could do without demeaning herself, if she was born in Florence early in the sixteenth century. Catherine had pondered upon a page in which Machiavelli discussed for the benefit of Lorenzo the Magnificent the good or bad use of cruelty: 'One can say that it is well used—if it is ever permissible to say that evil is good—if one has recourse to it but once, and for one's own security, and if in the end it is for the benefit of one's subjects.'

The Queen Mother thought that she was the best possible judge of her subjects' good. It could only come from the eradication of factions, and therefore, by good Italian standards, their leaders. As for the needs of her own safety, they had never seemed so pressing as since Coligny's return to Court, basking in the King's favour to the detriment of the King's mother and brother. Obviously, Coligny's murder was one of the political plans with which Catherine's mind and (if one can use the word here) conscience had long been obsessed. As early as 1563, she was already thinking of getting rid of Coligny, his brother d'Andelot and the Prince de Condé. A year later she revived the possibility of murdering the Admiral very freely (although in confidence) in discussion with the Duke of Ferrara, who later remembered her remarks and spoke of them.

The subject was revived in 1565 during the Franco-Spanish conference in Bayonne, this time between the Queen Mother and the Duke of Alva, and, it seems, so seriously that two years later Pius V, speaking to Philip II's ambassador, took for granted that it was still contemplated by the 'masters of France'. Finally, in 1569 it was all but done: Don Francis d'Alava, at that time the Spanish Ambassador to Charles IX, mentioned it three times to his master. It is true that at that time the Admiral had been tried in his absence as a rebel and that a parliamentary decree virtually legalized his murder in advance and promised a reward to his murderer in the King's name.

Yet at that time Coligny was perfectly safe in his own camp. Two known attempts on his life ended in failure. Dominique d'Albe, the Admiral's valet, who had been paid to poison him, was unmasked and executed at Faye-la-Vineuse on September 20th. As for Maurevert, as has already been said, he only succeeded in killing Coligny's first lieutenant, Louis de Vaudrey, Seigneur Mouy and St Phal.

One might be tempted to infer, and many have done so, that

if Catherine had taken the decision to have the Admiral assassinated in 1572, she had actually been considering it for ten years. Yet there are conflicting proofs which are equally reliable. If between 1563 and 1572 Catherine periodically thought of getting rid of Coligny, it is equally true that, during the same period, between the Peace of Amboise and the Peace of St Germain, she looked upon him as one of the major assets of her policy.

Thus it is possible to accept Pierre de Vaissiere's view,[1] that the Queen Mother, with perfect coolness, thought several times of having the Admiral murdered, then gave it up, then thought of it again, and finally came back to this plan in 1572: such a tortuous state of mind is revealing of the way in which Catherine, as Machiavelli's disciple, accepted his notion of necessary cruelty, probably without hate and in any case certainly without weakness. One can certainly go back to the middle of July 1572 to account for the attack of August 24th: the moment when the news of the disaster of Mons reached Paris and further aggravated the tension between supporters and opponents of intervention in the Netherlands.

Each day, the King used to closet himself with the Admiral for long talks. When they were over, if by any chance the Queen or the Duke of Anjou encountered Charles to speak to him of something only connected with his pleasures, they found him 'strikingly peevish and sullen'—that is, scarcely polite.[2] On one occasion Anjou even took fright. He entered his brother's room shortly after the Admiral had left. 'As soon as he saw me,' he wrote, 'he began furiously pacing up and down, not saying a word, but glaring at me often and sometimes putting his hand to his dagger in such a threatening way that I expected him to rush upon me and stab me.' The Duke cleverly managed to get to the door and then, opening it suddenly, 'bowed less respectfully than when he had entered' and slipped out, feeling it had been a narrow escape. He ran to his mother and both were persuaded that it was the Admiral who had given the King 'some evil and sinister idea' about them, and they henceforth decided to do all they could to get rid of him, discussing the matter with Mme de Nemours. One may remember that his

[1] P. de Vaissière, *De quelques assassins.*

[2] *Discours d'un personnage d'honneur et de qualité des causes et motifs de la St Barthélemy.*

lady's maiden name was Anne d'Este and she had never renounced the vendetta she had sworn against the Admiral after the death of Francis de Guise, her first husband. The Duke of Anjou gives no date for this ominous scene, but the Florentine Ambassador, Petrucci, in a letter to Francisco de' Medici, mentions mysterious meetings of the two great Italian ladies in the Court of France—the Queen and Mme de Nemours—the letter was dated July 23rd.

During the following days more plans were evolved and then abandoned. A 'Gascon captain' was summoned, who might have done the deed. But he proved to be so sure of himself and such a silly braggart—though he was probably brave—that he had to be given up. The ladies had a good laugh at him, listening to him and watching him while he acted the part with zest and a very strong Southern accent, posturing and showing how he would 'despatch the Admiral'.

According to the Viscomte de Turenne,[1] the next scheme was a sort of public execution by the young Duke de Guise in person on the occasion of a tilting match given by the King in the Louvre gardens, but it had to be abandoned, lest a blunder might cost the life of the King, Anjou or some other personage placed near Coligny. One had also to think of the possible reactions of some 500 Protestant noblemen who would be there.

Meanwhile, Coligny, as if he sensed the impending danger, had but one wish: to leave the Court and return to Chatillon, where the young wife he had married a year before was waiting for him. She was Jacqueline d'Entremont, his second wife, who, in order to marry 'a saint and a hero', had forfeited all her property and defied the anger of the powerful Duke of Savoy. Coligny wrote to her on August 18th:

'My very dear and well-beloved wife, today has been the wedding-day of the King's sister to the King of Navarre. The next three or four days will be wasted in games, banquets, masked balls and tournaments. The King has assured me he would then grant me a few days to take cognisance of complaints made in various places about the way in which the Edict of Pacification has been violated. . . . Though I long to see you, I am sure you would be sorry if I proved lazy over such a matter, and if things

[1] Duc de Bouillon, Vicomte de Turenne: *Mémoires*.

went wrong because I had not done my duty. Yet that will not long delay my departure from this place as I have leave to go next week. Were I to follow my own wish, I would feel much happier with you than staying longer here, for reasons I will tell you, but one must have more regard for public good than for one's private satisfaction.'

This letter was not intercepted by the Admiral's enemies, but everybody at Court knew, for Coligny made no secret of it, that when he wanted to discuss various matters connected with religion, the King had answered: 'Father, I want you to grant me four or five days only to amuse myself; after that, I promise you, as King, that I will make you happy, you and all those of your religion.'[1]

It was also known that some of Coligny's friends constantly implored him to return to Chatillon. A few of them, weary of vainly begging him to be careful, had left, rather publicizing their leave-taking. Among them was Blosset,[2] a Burgundian captain who had behaved extremely well in the Huguenot ranks at the siege of Vezelay; he came to say goodbye to the Admiral as early as August 20th.

'Why do you want to leave so soon?' inquired Coligny.

'Because no one wishes you well here.'

'What do you mean? Rest assured we have a good king....'

'He is too good,' replied Blosset. 'That is why I want to leave. And if you were to do the same, it would be better for yourself and for us.'

As for Langoiran, after having also tried in vain to convince the Admiral, he had left, telling all and sundry: 'I am going; I would rather look a madman than stay among fools.'

Consequently, plotters had to act at once to prevent the Admiral from bringing to the King's notice the way in which the Edict had been violated, and also to forestall his departure, which would put him out of reach.

It was then that Charles de Louviers reappeared at the suggestion of the Duchess of Nemours: Lord of Maurevert, Knight of the Order of St Michel, he was immediately accepted as 'the proper and experienced instrument of the murder', according

[1] Pierre de L'Estoile; *op. cit.*

[2] Louis de Blosset, lord de Fleury. He had fought under Coligny at Poitiers and La Roche-Abeille; he was with Henri de Navarre at Coutras in 1587.

to Anjou. Catherine, who had brushed aside all counter-suggestions, approved the choice without hesitation. Maurevert, in fact, completely satisfied her, and not only by reason of his sinister competence. He was exactly what the Queen Mother needed when she had made up her mind to act with the Guises: Maurevert, when a page, had been a retainer of the house of Lorraine, and everybody knew that he maintained close contact with his former masters. Moreover, he was going to benefit in preparing and carrying out his attack by the material provided by the Lorraine princes: first of all he was given a lodging, the tenant of which, Pierre de Piles de Villemur, was one of Henri de Guise's former tutors. The lodging was well situated: Rue des Fossés-St-Germain,[1] on the route Coligny followed each day when he walked from his house in the Rue de Béthisy[2] to the Louvre and back.

So the plot hatched between the Queen Mother and her two secret Italian councillors, the Florentine, Albert de Gondi, Comte de Retz, and the Milanese René de Birague, Keeper of the Seals, was going to be realized. The Admiral was to be shot dead by an arquebuse in full daylight, from a house which would be easily identified as belonging to a servant of the Guises. The Protestants would not fail to hurl themselves upon the Lorraines, but the Parisians would intervene against the Huguenots. The upshot would be a battle during which the two extreme factions would slay each other. And the King's men, massed in the Louvre, would be ready to act at a convenient time to crush the party that remained in control of the field. Simon Goulart[3] gives a minute account of that plan: it was quite worthy of Machiavelli, and he adds that it seemed 'the most expedient way possible'. Yet it would all have to unfold exactly as Catherine, Anjou and the Italians had planned. . . .

An arquebuse misfires

Maurevert was thus installed in the Rue des Fossés-St-Germain.

[1] Now Rue Perrault.

[2] The Rue de Bethisy was a continuation of the Rue des Fossés-St-Germain. The site of Coligny's house, at the corner of the Rue de l'Arbre-Sec, is now No. 144 of the Rue de Rivoli. The old building has been pulled down.

[3] 1543-1629. Lawyer and theologian. He studied in Geneva, then went back to France as a pastor in 1572; he escaped alive from the massacre. Later he was a pastor in the Forez and in Grenoble. He wrote a great deal and published chronicles of his time.

Villemur, the tenant, had conveniently left on a journey a few days before, and the supervisor of Guise's household, François de Villiers, Seigneur de Chailly, came in person to introduce Maurevert to his maid as a certain 'Bondot, a horseman and archer in the King's guard' and one of her master's dear friends.

The pseudo-Bondot and his servants were well received and comfortably lodged and well fed and wined; for three days he remained there, never stirring from the house. He made a note of the times when Coligny passed the house, going to the Louvre or coming back, so as to get accustomed to his habits and to be able without hesitation to distinguish him from his usual companions.

On the morning of the 22nd he was ready. While his servant went to give warning to Chailly, who had horses ready, Maurevert went down to the ground floor and settled himself at a grated window and hiding behind the washing drying on a line. His gun rested on the window sill, with scarcely an inch or two protruding. Now, the Admiral could come.

But he did not come. At least, not yet. . . .

The council had been presided over by Monsieur, the Duke of Anjou, and it had not been longer than usual. But something happened which Maurevert could not know: as Coligny was about to leave he was met by the King who was returning from Mass. He was in an excellent humour and he took Coligny along with him to the tennis court. Coligny had to watch the King play. He was partnering Henri de Guise, and their adversaries were Charles de Téligny, the Admiral's son-in-law, and one of his friends.

It was therefore shortly after eleven when the little group Maurevert was expecting came out of the Rue des Poulies.[1] The Admiral was walking first, between Guerchy and de Sorbier. In all there were about a dozen Protestant noblemen, among whom were Piles,[2] Monneins, de Moustier, Cornaton, St Auban,[3] de Séré and Barnaud;[4] they were walking slowly, chattering in

---

[1] Where the east pavement of the Rue du Louvre now stands.

[2] Armand de Clermont, Baron de Piles, a young outstanding leader. He fought under Condé in Orleans in 1562, then at la Roche-Abeille, St Jean d'Amgély, etc. He had come to Paris with Jeanne d'Albret.

[3] Jacques Pape, Lord of St Auban. He had been Coligny's page. Two days later he saved his life by pretending to become a Catholic, escaped out of Paris, fought in the Dauphiny in 1573, and was wounded in 1574. He was still alive in 1594.

[4] Nicolas Barnaud. See p. 103.

hushed voices so as not to disturb the Admiral who, while walking, was glancing at a report which had just been handed him.

Suddenly, Coligny made an unexpected gesture. Later, he said that 'he turned round to spit'. 'He stooped to readjust his slipper,' said another. Whatever he did, his action coincided almost to the second with Maurevert's shot, with the result that instead of wounding him in the chest—for the aim was good —the two bullets, which should have 'despatched' him, wounded him in the right hand and the left forearm.

Despite the pain which convulsed his thin ascetic face, he reacted at once as a great party leader should. His first words had a deep political implication:

'Thus are honest people treated in France!'

While Guerchy and Sorbier were supporting him and improvising some sort of dressing with a handkerchief, several of their companions rushed into the house whence the shot had been fired, and which had been pointed out by Coligny himself: it was easy to detect it, as smoke was still rising.

The door resisted them and they lost time. When they burst it open, they found the arquebuse thrown upon a bed in a room on the ground floor: it was still hot. A heavy purse, which lay on a table, proved that the murderer was not short of money.

Villemur's servant and 'Bondot's' valet told what they knew: the murderer, as soon as his shots had been fired, had jumped on a horse which was waiting for him, fully saddled, in the cloister of St Germain l' Auxerrois, at the other entrance of the house. The man was easy to recognize, on account of his large grey cloak. He had been in such a hurry, and possibly in such terror, that he had made three attempts to hoist himself into the saddle.

While the first investigations were made, Coligny, who had refused to be carried, walked home, assisted by two friends. He had sent Piles and Monneins to the Louvre to break the news to the King; a third man had hurried to fetch the surgeon, Ambroise Paré, who, with inadequate instruments, inflicted excruciating pain upon his patient while amputating the shattered finger of the right hand and extracting the bullet which had lodged itself in the left elbow. During the operation, the Pastor Merlin,[1] in whom Coligny had full confidence, never left his bedside.

[1] See p. 76.

In the Louvre Charles IX was still playing tennis when Piles and Monneins ran in panting. Coligny had reacted as a political leader; but the King behaved like a bad-mannered child, disturbed while at play and angered at the thought that the crime was going to inconvenience him. He threw down his racket with a peevish gesture, swearing and shouting: 'What, more trouble? Shall I never have any peace?'

It was some time before he thought to ask how the Admiral was and whether he was badly wounded.

It certainly seems that such clumsy behaviour can be regarded as proof of his surprise, and that he knew nothing of his mother and his brother's plot. Those who believed—and still believe—that he was party to the attack of August 22nd, forget that spontaneous reaction. Had it been the contrary, he probably would have been more careful and not so true to himself, especially before Protestants.

How different was the Queen Mother's reaction! She had much more control over her feelings, but she had no need to dissemble so much since she was surrounded by none but her own people. She was at lunch when she was told, not that the Admiral had been murdered—which was what she expected—but that the attempt had failed. She turned very pale, remained a moment as if stupefied, then rose without a word and shut herself in her room.

Meanwhile the news began to spread through Paris and everybody heard of the shot and its poor result. The registers and chronicles of the city offices mention the orders dispatched to the 'archers, bowmen and arquebusiers of the said city' by the end of the morning, ordering them to muster their companies, arm them and take them to the City Hall. The officers of the city militia for their part were requested to reinforce the watches at the city gates, to check people coming in or going out, while preventing citizens from taking up arms and shopkeepers from putting up their shutters.

At the Louvre the Princes, Henri de Navarre and his young cousin Condé, both Huguenots, came to the King, demanding audience and calling for justice. Charles received them in the presence of Catherine, and his anger was perfectly genuine.

'I swear and promise,' he shouted, 'to inflict such condign punishment on the culprits, their accomplices, aiders and abetters, that the Admiral and his friends will be satisfied.'

Catherine could not hear such an oath without shuddering, but she could not afford to look less resolute than her son, and she too denounced 'the insult offered to the King'. She was in deadly terror and she would not move from the King's side. She was near him when Téligny and Damville (one of the Montmorency brothers and the Chatillons' cousin) brought word to the King that the Admiral was in no condition to leave his house, but wished nevertheless to speak to him.

Charles replied at once: 'Tell my father, the Admiral, that I shall visit him in person.'

Catherine dreaded above all to leave the Admiral alone with the King: it might prove fatal for her and Anjou. Accordingly she requested Téligny and Damville, whom she surprised very much, to tell the Admiral that she would be coming too.

Meanwhile, what had happened to Louviers de Maurevert? Later, Anjou was to say, with a mixture of anger and contempt, that he had proved neither so good nor so sure a shot as was thought.

Two Protestant noblemen, St Auban and Séré, had left their companions breaking in the door of Villemur's house, and had led Coligny home. Then they rushed in pursuit of the murderer. His track was easy to follow, as Maurevert, who was quite certain that his shot had been successful, had not been able to resist shouting to the people he met, while galloping towards the St Antoine Gate: 'The Admiral is dead! France has an Admiral no longer!'

St Auban has written an account of his pursuit.[1] At Charenton he and Séré arrested a servant of Maurevert's uncle: the man had been waiting for the killer with a fresh horse, and had taken from him the grey cloak which he had been wearing in his frantic flight. Their ride took them to Melun, under the walls of the castle of Chailly-en-Bière: the drawbridge was up and the loopholes bristling with primed guns, forbidding anybody to come near. St Auban and his companion knew enough: they got back to Paris the next day and told their friends who had aided and abetted the murderer.

'*The pain is mine*'

By the end of that afternoon, the Protestants knew all they

[1] Jacques Pape, Seigneur de St Auban, *Mémoires*.

49

needed to know; they had easily identified the gun as coming from the armoury of Anjou's bodyguard. They had no difficulty in connecting Villemur, Chailly and their master Guise. And if they were not quite sure of the murderer's identity, they had a choice between two names only: Maurevert, or a Florentine *bravo* in the pay of the Queen and Anjou, Pietro-Paolo Tosinghi.

So it was with a mixture of surprise and anger that they saw the strange company escorting the King when he called on the Admiral: Catherine and her two other sons, and, among the lords in attendance, not only the Marshals Damville, Cossé, Tavannes and the Princes of the blood, but also the three Italian councillors of the Queen Mother—Retz, Nevers and Birague, whose hatred for Coligny was only too well known. In fact, only the Guises were missing.

'Sire,' said Coligny, sitting up in bed; 'I humbly thank you for the honour it pleases Your Majesty to pay me and for all the trouble you are taking on my behalf. . . .'

Charles IX protested his affection for the Admiral, asked whether he was in great pain and praised his courage; then Coligny went on talking. Ignoring the presence of his worst enemies, he made a long public declaration which had the importance of a political testament, for the speaker (who could not know if the bullets had been poisoned or not) might die in a few hours. He justified his past attitude, denounced the traitors who were daily betraying to the Duke of Alva all that was discussed in council (the traitors were there, listening to him) mentioned numerous violations of the Edict of Pacification and gave recent instances.

The King listened intently, agreeing and sometimes putting in a word, as if to defend himself; finally he referred again to the attempted murder:

'If the wound is yours, the pain is mine. God's death! I will avenge this outrage in such a way that it will be remembered for ever!'

'Sire,' Coligny replied softly, 'it is not necessary to look very far for he who did me this service. Just ask M. de Guise: he may tell you.'

A discussion then began between them in a low voice, which infuriated Catherine, who could not catch a single word. In despair, and on the pretext that fatigue was likely to make the wounded man worse, she motioned everybody to the door, to the King's great displeasure; obviously, he wanted to hear everything the Admiral had to say.

When the Court had left, the Protestants who had gathered in the Rue de Béthisy held a last council. Navarre, Condé, La Rochefoucauld[1] wanted to take security measures at once. Jean de Ferrières, Vidame de Chartres,[2] went even further: according to him, the Admiral must leave Paris that very evening, despite his wounds. But Téligny reminded them of the King's words and his obviously sincere anger against the murderers, however highly situated they were. In fact, the Admiral's son-in-law was vouching for the King who had offered royal protection to the wounded man and his friends: had he not even insisted that Coligny be carried to the Louvre and cared for in the Royal apartments? Finally, Ambroise Paré said that he could guarantee nothing if the patient left his bed.

Téligny's suggestion was accepted, and the Protestants left the Admiral's lodgings in little groups. Those who remained with the wounded man were his family, his servants, the surgeon, Merlin and a few noblemen to guard him.

In the Louvre, at that very moment, the atmosphere had suddenly become overheated. Catherine and Anjou had scarcely left Coligny before they urged the King to tell them what had been so secretly confided to him. Charles at first refused to reply, then suddenly, pressed further, he turned on his mother in an outburst of anger:

'What the Admiral told me is true. In France, Kings are only recognized by the power they wield. Now this power has drifted entirely into your hands, and the authority you display in my stead may some day be very detrimental to me and my kingdom. He told me to hold it in suspicion and to be on my guard against it, and to take great care, and that he wanted to warn me, as one of my most faithful subjects and servants, before he died. God's death! You wanted to know! Well, that's what the Admiral told me!'

---

[1] François de la Rochefoucauld. Fought at Metz in 1552, then at Dreux with Condé, under whose influence he had become a Protestant.

[2] 1521(?)-1584. Fought under Guise at Metz but became a Protestant when he was still very young. Took part in the Conspiracy of Amboise. Went to England in 1562 to negotiate, again in 1570, and also in 1572, after he had escaped from Paris. He fought under Condé and Navarre and died in prison.

Dumbfounded with rage, Catherine left the King, who locked himself in his study with his secretary. By the end of that dramatic day the Queen was faced with the utter collapse of all her plans. She knew that the King was sending orders to speed the inquiry into the attempted murder. He had promised Coligny that Cavaignes and Masperault, whom the Admiral completely trusted, were to be appointed as judges together with de Thou, Morsan and Viole. Then, doubtless, the Guises would be indicted and Catherine well knew that they would not fail to betray her at once, together with Anjou, her adored son. The latter was with her and unable to suggest anything. He could only, from time to time, swear to make that clumsy Maurevert suffer the worst conceivable tortures.

Catherine was alone, more lonely than she had ever been. She had to find a loophole before the morrow. For the present, as Anjou noticed, they were both 'devoid of plans or intelligence'. So mother and son decided—and the terrible word was written by Anjou—to postpone the 'party' until the next day.

CHAPTER TWO

Saint Bartholomew's Eve

THE night had been quiet. Paris had not stirred. Neither the Protestants nor the Guises had created any disturbance. At dawn, Coligny's friends met at his bedside; the Admiral had slept well, he did not look feverish and they all waited confidently for Ambroise Paré's verdict.

The surgeon probed the wounds, applied a new dressing, sounded his patient's heart and felt his pulse, and said at last: 'The wounds are doing well. The Admiral's life is in no danger whatever; his arm may lose some of its strength, but it will heal all right.'

Téligny was delighted: had he not been listened to, had the Vidame de Chartres' suggestion been accepted and the Admiral removed to Chatillon the night before, he would not have been so well in the morning. Another fact had to be taken into account, which was of the greatest moment for Coligny: by not leaving Paris he had shown how completely they trusted the King, who would show his appreciation. As the day which was dawning might be decisive, the Admiral counselled his friends to be prudent and moderate.

'I beg you not to attempt anything and not to try to take up arms to avenge this,' he said. 'It would only make our cause odious just when our enemies have blundered so seriously that they cannot be ignored. Let us just watch the King, for he has solemnly promised to do quick and exemplary justice.'

And it was true that when Téligny went to the Louvre a little later to bring news of the Admiral to the King, Charles IX greeted him with apparently genuine pleasure. He wanted to know the very words Ambroise Paré had used and whether he was certain that there was no question of amputating the arm, and he finally said to Téligny:

53

'I am very pleased with your news. I hope the Admiral will soon be well again to do me signal service.'

At the same time, messengers were posting from one relay to another, bearing letters which the King had dictated the night before to the governors and to ambassadors beyond the frontiers. In them Charles IX disclosed, especially to Schomberg and La Mothe-Fénelon, who were his representatives in Germany and England, the attempt that had been made upon Coligny's life, expressing his own anger and adding that it was a crime which could almost certainly be imputed to the Guises, and that he was resolved to have justice done at once.

As for the Protestant leaders in Paris, they had also sent messengers to their friends in the provinces. In accordance with Coligny's orders, they asked them 'neither to act nor to show displeasure at what had been done to the Admiral, as God and the King were powerful enough to take vengence; that justice was already afoot against the culprit and his accomplices; and finally that, thanks to God, the wounds were not fatal; an arm was hurt but not the brain'.

'I can soon catch them again. . . .'

Early in the morning Catherine and Anjou too had learned that Coligny was not likely to get worse. They were told of Téligny's visit to the King and they also knew what had taken place in the Rue de Béthisy, as the Queen had a spy among the Protestants. This spy was Bayancourt, Seigneur de Bouchavannes, young Condé's tutor.[1] Through Charlotte de Sauve, one of the most crafty and less prudish members of her 'flying squad' of beauties, Catherine knew the contents of the King's letters. Charlotte's husband, Simon de Fizes, was one of the King's secretaries whose loyalty he had very good reason to suspect.

Mother and son also knew that the King did not doubt that the Guises were guilty. Something happened during the morning, of which they heard at once; it turned their fright into sheer panic. Shortly after Charles IX's friendly talk with Téligny, Henri de Guise and his uncle Aumale—speaking in the absence of the Cardinal of Lorraine, then in Rome, and in the name of Francis' brothers—entered the Louvre with a party of retainers

---

[1] Antoine de Bayancourt had been perfectly loyal to the elder Condé and had fought well at Jarnac. His attitude was far less straightforward later. He was still alive in 1588.

and begged an audience of the King. Charles saw them at once, with a heavy frown on his face. The Duke of Aumale began thus:

'It seems as if your Majesty has for some time been pleased to disapprove of our services and might possibly be glad to see us leave his court and go back to our estates.'

The King, scarcely concealing his anger, answered curtly: 'God's death! You may go to the devil, for all I care!'

And, as soon as the young Duke and his uncle had left, the King went on in a loud voice: 'They may go where they please! I shall soon catch them again, if it is proved they are guilty of what has been done to the Admiral.'

When the council met a few moments later, the one subject under discussion was the inquiry into the crime and the account of the judges' first findings. Among the judges were two of the Admiral's personal friends, who had been appointed immediately after the King's visit to his bedside. A warrant had been issued against Chailly, but it had not been possible to arrest him as the Guises had put him beyond reach of the law. Yet the evidence of Villemur's servant and 'Bondot's' valet had been taken. The valet arrested by St Auban at Charenton had talked; the description of the murderer had made it possible to identify Maurevert. The origin of the gun had been fully established.

So the net was closing around the Guises and also, inevitably, around the Queen and Anjou. Things were developing at such a pace that it looked as if the day would not end before the King's blind fury would lead him to fateful decisions: the arrest of Henri de Guise and of his mother, whose confessions would implicate Catherine and her son. Who could tell what might follow? The King's insane jealousy of his brother might drive him to hand Anjou over to the judges and then to the executioner, and to banish the Queen from France for ever. Had not Machiavelli written: 'One must be a fox to know the snares, and a lion to frighten the wolves.'?

Catherine, by temperament, might have wished to be only a fox. But now it was too late, for the wolves were hot on her trail and snarling for the blood of the son she loved best. To save him, and to save herself, she had to become a lioness. Going one step further than her Florentine master, she was going to do more than frighten the wolves.

Paris warms up

The Queen was bound to act at once. Making no pretence at standing on her dignity, she decided to keep to the tactics which had proved successful the day before: she called on the King, knowing that in spite of his anger he would not dare to send her away. Thus she would know what was being discussed and organized, and she might be able, as she had already done once, to parry her enemies' thrust.

She had hardly arrived at the King's apartments with Anjou when Téligny and Cornaton, Coligny's envoys, called again. They were coming to complain to the King of a suspicious gathering of armed men which puzzled the Admiral very much: so much so that he was asking for the King's protection.

'What does this mean?' wondered the King. 'Are my people rebelling and taking up arms?'

'Neither one thing nor the other,' Catherine hurriedly put in. 'Don't you remember that you ordered the City Council to have guards in readiness in each district in case there was trouble?'

'That is true . . . Yet, I forbade them to carry weapons. Anyhow, I want the Admiral's house to be guarded.'

Anjou, realizing the potential advantages of such a decision, took up his cue at once:

'By all means . . . Take Cosseins and fifty arquebusiers.'

Jean de Monlezun de Cosseins, one of the three colonels of the King's guards, was a veteran of the Italian wars and was devoted body and soul to the Guises. His very name made Coligny's envoys shudder, but it was too late to refuse, as the King had already agreed to his brother's choice of the man and the size of the detachment. One of the envoys vainly attempted to raise a protest.

'We would be quite satisfied with six archers of your own guard: their authority would do more to keep the mob away than a larger group of men from a different unit.'

But Anjou insisted and the King, who considered the matter settled, was giving other orders. His quartermasters would find lodgings round St Germain l'Auxerrois and the Rue de Béthisy for the largest possible number of Protestants: the Admiral's safety would then be greater. If necessary, one might ask the Catholics living near the Admiral's lodging to go elsewhere. . . . Téligny and Cornaton were more convinced than ever of the

King's good intentions, though they were slightly perturbed by Anjou's intervention. Yet they thanked Charles and left. They had scarcely left the King's chamber when one of the witnesses of the scene, Thoré,[1] Montmorency's brother and therefore Coligny's cousin, whispered into their ears: 'You could not have given yourselves into the care of a greater enemy!'

However, it was by no means pointless to protect the Admiral, for Paris was growing restless. To begin with, contrary to what they had told the King, Guise and Aumale were not leaving for their estates. They had left the Louvre surrounded by a numerous retinue and had actually taken the direction of the St Antoine Gate but, on reaching the Rue du Chaume,[2] had turned left and gone home to the former Manor of Clisson, where the Dukes of Bedford and Clarence lived during the English occupation of Paris. Anne d'Este had bought the palace and it was now the Guise mansion. Then the gates were firmly closed as if to withstand a siege.

Meanwhile, the most contradictory rumours began to circulate in Paris, where the Guise retainers and the Catholic preachers had not remained inactive. They had told the people of Paris (though it was not true) that the King had asked the Marshal de Montmorency to come and occupy the centre of the capital with large cavalry and infantry contingents. Now Montmorency was a kinsman of Coligny and a traditional enemy of the Guises. The truth was that Francis de Montmorency, much too wary to get himself involved in these new troubles, had left the day before, telling everybody he was going to hunt on his estates near l'Isle-Adam.

Anger was growing on the Huguenot side too. The perpetrators of the crime committed against Coligny included the Queen and Anjou and they were so well known by now that most noblemen refused to obey the Admiral's request for patience and quiet. In front of his house, some of them were clamouring for revenge. 'This arm,' some were saying, 'is worth thirty thousand other arms.' A few armed horsemen, shouting threats, rode past the heavily locked gates and barred shutters of the Guises' house. Of course, those incidents were echoed,

---

[1] The youngest of the Montmorency brothers. He became a Protestant later on and fought side by side with Henri de Navarre.
[2] Now Rue des Archives.

distorted and exaggerated and only increased the exasperation of the Catholic population of Paris. And as the majority of people were not working, since it was the eve of the feast day of St Bartholomew, apostle and martyr, and a public holiday in the diocese of Paris, groups formed round 'improvised', though carefully trained, speakers who knew just how to turn on the heat a little more.

In the Tuileries Gardens

It was midday and nothing irretrievable had yet occurred. Catherine was at last able to pass over to the offensive.

She had a few free hours during which she could relax her supervision: as usual, Charles was going to spend the early afternoon with his mistress. Though Marie Touchet was a Huguenot, the Queen Mother did not dread this interview too much. She knew that what her son liked in the girl above all was her complete indifference to everything other than their love. With her the King could forget the worries and anxieties which a moment earlier had fed his anger.

While Charles basked in Marie's love, Catherine matured her battle plan. This time, she was going to make sure that success did not slip through her fingers due to some minute hitch. A gunman's clumsiness was not going to wreck the enterprise this time.

No longer did she aim at an isolated localized deed. It was going to be a decisive trial of strength, from which Catherine would emerge victorious or annihilated. She had reached a decision, and she merely needed the means to carry it out. Consequently, she summoned her most intimate councillors to the Tuileries, those on whom she could wholly rely, not only because they owed her everything (which would not be enough to guarantee their loyalty) but because they knew that their fate was closely and definitely linked to hers. Anjou, who was already her accomplice, was waiting with her: he was aware that she was working as much for him as for herself. The others were her three Italians, Nevers, Gondi, Birague, and a Frenchman, Gaspard de Saulx-Tavannes, Marshal of France, who was utterly devoted to Anjou and of whose loyalty Catherine had already found proof in many circumstances. As early as 1556, he had come to her in great earnest, offering to cut off the nose of her husband's mistress, Diane de Poitiers. According to

Tavannes himself, Catherine thanked him but said that she preferred 'to wait in patience'.[1]

To this well-tested devotion was added the fact that Tavannes was a relentless enemy of Coligny and all Huguenots. He had lately displayed his hatred when, at the King's council, Coligny had returned to the subject of the war in the Netherlands. Tavannes had never been able to forgive the way in which Coligny had then insulted him, saying: 'He who is against the war with Spain is not a good Frenchman and has a red cross in his belly.'

The councillors arrived discreetly, one after the other, as if summoned to a conspiracy—which is exactly what it was. Catherine, who was fearful even of the walls of her own palace, took them into the gardens: they would be safer there, away from possible spies. The discussion was brief; they were all agreed as to what was necessary, to have the Admiral despatched, one way or another. They were also unanimous on another subject, which was more delicate and which was roundly summed up by Anjou, who always went straight to the point: 'It is no longer possible to use tricks and cunning; it will have to be done in the open. But in order to do that one must bring the King to this way of thinking.'

Catherine and her accomplices were well aware that this was easier said than done. Each of them suggested arguments which might win the King's support, yet one thing remained to be done: select the one who was to put them to Charles with some hope of getting them heard. Finally, it seems that they all agreed to entrust it to Gondi, Comte de Retz. He was a Florentine like Catherine, and his bad influence had been powerful on the King since childhood.

Gondi was to talk to the King late in the evening, so that he would have no time left to change his mind; and when the King had been sufficiently 'prepared' by this talk, Catherine and the others would come in and finish what he had begun. They never thought they might fail: either the King would give in, or he would no longer be King except in name. In fact, it was on this last hidden threat that the Queen relied most. If Gondi felt hesitant to speak it, she would do so herself.

The secret council came to an end. While Gondi was learning his part, a new visitor was ushered in, and he was going to

[1] Gaspard de Saulx-Tavannes, *Mémoires.*

59

provide them with a few more arguments: this was Boucha-vannes. He had come straight from the Rue de Béthisy. He had much to tell about what was happening there, probably embellished in order to make himself more welcome. He had noticed the growing anger of the Protestants and this was playing into the Queen's hand. If necessary, one might make up a tale about a Huguenot plot to avenge the Admiral, of which the victims would be the Guises, but also Anjou and the Queen Mother, and—why not?—the King himself.

In the Rue de Béthisy

It was true that on the Protestant side men like Téligny or Briquemault, who attempted to soothe the spirits of the rest, were listened to less and less. There were very good reasons, especially the presence of Cosseins and his fifty men in the immediate proximity of Coligny's lodgings. This was the detachment sent by the King to protect Coligny, 'for fear', the King had said, 'that anyone may cause him displeasure'.

Now Cosseins was notoriously one of the Huguenots' bitterest enemies; not only that, but from the moment he had arrived in the Rue de Bethisy several incidents had occurred which revealed the way in which this strange protector intended to discharge his duty.

One of Téligny's pages had been ordered by his master to bring two spears to the Admiral's lodgings: Cosseins forbade it and confiscated them. The King of Navarre had to leave Coligny's bedside and go down in person to argue with Cosseins and bring in the page and the weapons. Shortly afterwards, there was a further squabble: Cosseins, 'seeing Téligny's and Guerchy's cuirasses brought to the Admiral's lodgings, drove away those who were carrying them'.

'Guerchy, a warrior, who was quick with his sword, hearing of what had happened, went to Cosseins and roundly abused him, and they would have fought but for Téligny, who was a sweet-tempered gentleman as everybody knew, and who talked pleasantly to them and calmed them.'[1]

Cosseins' attitude was well-meant to irritate and disturb the Protestants; and the stream of news, both true and false, which kept pouring in, was not of the kind to reassure them. Some Huguenots came in to report that about four in the afternoon

---

[1] Simon Goulart, op. cit.

they had seen Guise and his bastard brother, Angoulême, driving through Paris and practically reviewing the town militia which had gathered in arms, contrary to the King's orders. They had noticed that after the parade dangerous rumours likely to exasperate the already overheated Parisian mob had been spread all over the place—the story of Montmorency occupying Paris with his troops, for instance. A little later, the Admiral's trumpeter ran in, almost distracted with terror. Passing the Louvre, he had just seen men carrying heavy bundles of weapons into the Palace courtyard. Could it mean that some plot was being hatched against the Protestants?

Once more, Téligny calmed them: who knew better than himself—as he was to take part in them—that joustings were being prepared inside the courtyard of the Louvre? A castle had even been erected which was to be stormed by the jousters. Obviously, the weapons were intended for these games. Since the attack on the Admiral, Téligny had never ceased to defend the King and his good faith, and to stand as guarantee of his good intentions. But his companions were weary of his optimism and they took his explanations rather coolly.

A few Protestant lords who had come to Paris for Navarre's wedding and were now coming to the Rue de Béthisy to hear the news, made no secret of their distrust of the King of Navarre: he was too closely tied to the Valois now, and already contaminated by the corrupt morals of that court of which they had not known until then and which had shocked their puritanism. Yet it must be admitted that Navarre's attitude, during those last hours, had been irreproachable. He had not left the Admiral except, in company with Condé, to go to make a protest to the King. And, to show how much he distrusted Cosseins, he had just summoned five of his own Swiss guards to keep watch through the night inside Coligny's house. As for his young wife, the beautiful Margot, she too had displayed great devotion towards the Admiral, visiting him several times, though she knew she had few friends in his house and might expect some hostility from his followers, for she was still the 'Popish Princess' in spite of her marriage. In thus displaying a sympathy she did not feel in the least, she was obeying the King her brother as much as her husband. Indeed, Charles continuously requested those around him to go and call on the Admiral and keep him company, and on several occasions he was anxious to know if his orders had been carried out and if steps had been taken to house Huguenot noblemen near Coligny's lodgings.

M. de Rambouillet, his quartermaster, had done all he could to obey him. He had had apartments cleared for them in various inns in the vicinity and also in private houses. Many Protestants had thus been able to move in during the day. They had done so without grumbling since it was 'for the Admiral's safety', and yet in spite of the quartermaster's exertion some of them were rather badly housed. Jean de Mergey,[1] a nobleman from Champagne in the Comte de la Rochefoucauld's retinue, wrote in a dispirited way that 'the count left his apartment to move into one set aside for him, where he found neither host nor hostess nor furniture'.

All these removals had been completed by the end of the day. Yet not all the Protestant noblemen had abandoned their comforts—or their own safety—with the zeal of La Rochefoucauld. A certain number, especially Henri de Navarre's retainers, remained in the Louvre. A few others, some sixty of them, who were feeling rather suspicious, refused to stay in the city, in spite of every entreaty, and they kept answering that the air was purer outside the gates in the open fields.[2] Sully mentioned some of them: he was barely thirteen in 1572, but he was directly involved in the events. He mentioned Montmorency, Frontenay, Rabodanges, le Brueil, Ségur, Sey, le Touchet, des Hayes, St Gelais, Choupes, Beauvais, Grandy, St Etienne, d'Armes, Bois-Sec and others from Normandy and Poitou. Most of them went to the Faubourg St Germain. By day they were within a few minutes of the Louvre, thanks to the many ferrymen; at night, as the heavy gate of Buci was locked and barred, they experienced some relief at feeling out of the trap, ready to 'get across country' as the brothers Caumont and La Force, whom Sully forgot to put down on his list, said.

The fateful evening

It was at the end of that Saturday, August 23rd, that the responsibilities, so far as History is concerned, were about to be settled. That is why the day and the hour mark the beginning of

---

[1] Jean de Mergey, *Mémoires.*

[2] *Mémoires des sages et royales Oeconomies d'Estat, domestiques, politiques et militaires de Henry le Grand.*

the widest disagreements between the witnesses, who were often also the actors in the tragedy.

If one is to believe Marguerite, Queen of Navarre—and there is no reason why not, for she really was, as Michelet says, 'the great, truthful naïve historian of the St Bartholomew massacre' —the Queen Mother, grasping the opportunity of a brief moment of privacy with the King, began to try and work on his feelings, not waiting for Gondi's intervention.

Keeping to the official version which held the Guises responsible for the crime of the previous day, Catherine sought to excuse Duke Henri, who 'had not received justice for the Admiral's assassination of his own father, and had wanted to take revenge'. Charles listened without a word. Emboldened, the Queen went on, adding that Coligny, on the whole, had well deserved such treatment. She herself still mourned a trusted servant, Charry, an officer in the King's guard, who had faithfully served her during her regency and the King's minority and who had been murdered by one of the Chatillons' hired assassins.

In spite of the very real power she still held over her son, her perfect acting and the tears she shed over the devoted Charry —a name she had not mentioned for a long time—Charles did not weaken:

'God's death!' he replied. 'I ordered that M. de Guise should be apprehended. I will not tolerate that such a crime should go unpunished.'

Dinner was presently served and it prevented the Queen from having to pursue the matter after such an awkward beginning. Charles had no time to add that an inquest, held immediately after Charry's death, had not produced the slightest proof that the Chatillons had been its instigators. Besides, everybody knew that Charry, shortly before his death, had murdered the brother of Chatelier Portault, his own eventual murderer, in cold blood.

This convenient supper provided Catherine with new arguments. Exasperation had been increasing among the Protestant noblemen all day and it was vented with some heat in the King's presence by some of them: all witnesses agree on that point. Among them was Armand de Clermont, Seigneur de Piles,[1] a

---

[1] He was a very young man when he began service under Louis de Condé in Orleans in 1562. In 1569 he fought in the South of France and was in Jeanne d'Albret's retinue when she came to Paris in 1572. He had married Jeanne de Durfort. Their two sons were both killed on battlefields when very young, before 1594.

courageous officer who had fought with outstanding bravery against the Royal army at St Jean d'Angély, but who had meanwhile made his peace with the King, so that on that very morning he had bathed in the Seine with the King, 'holding him under the chin to teach him to swim'.[1] Clermont said in a loud voice, staring into the Queen Mother's face, that 'if justice is not done to them within twenty-four hours, the Huguenots in Paris will see to it themselves'. Hector de Pardaillan Gondrin,[2] going a step further, added that 'if the Admiral were to lose an arm, a thousand others would be raised to effect such a massacre that the kingdom's rivers would run with blood'.

Such boastings were meant as a challenge to the Guise party, and they were also aimed at Anjou and his mother. Yet Catherine, while pretending to be shocked that anyone should dare to raise his voice in this way at the King's table, was already musing on the clever use she would make of those silly blunders.

The siege of the King

Gondi's intervention took place shortly after dinner. The Florentine was about fifty: he was part favourite and part tutor to the King, and Brantôme, who does not mince words, wrote that 'he taught the King every perversion'.

There is no doubt that Gondi had asked for a private audience with the King before the council arranged for the evening, and that he made every effort to get the King to side with the decisions taken in the afternoon in the Tuileries. Both Tavannes and Marguerite de Valois have attributed a decisive efficacy to this interview. Yet it should be observed that Anjou does not mention it. It is true that the author of the *Discours d'une personne d'honneur et de qualité* is suspiciously silent about Gondi, as we shall see. Marguerite clearly states that the Queen Mother had resolved to have everything put to the King by M. de Retz (Gondi), 'as she knew that he was more likely to be heard than anyone else, since Retz was the King's most intimate confidant and favourite'.

So Gondi went to the King's study at about nine that evening. What arguments did the wily Florentine use to change the King's mind completely? He began by striking such a powerful

[1] Brantôme.
[2] Three Pardaillan brothers were Protestants and two were killed in 1572.

3   CHARLES IX. School of Clouet   (*Musée du Louvre*)

CATHERINE DE' MEDICI. School of Clouet   (*Musée du Louvre*)

4

(left)
HENRI,
PRINCE
DE CONDÉ
Contemporary
drawing
(*Musée
du Louvre*)

(right)
HENRI,
DUC DE GUISE
(*Bibliotheque
Nationale*)

5   CONTEMPORARY MAP OF THE SCENE OF THE MASSACRE

(Studios Josse Lalance)

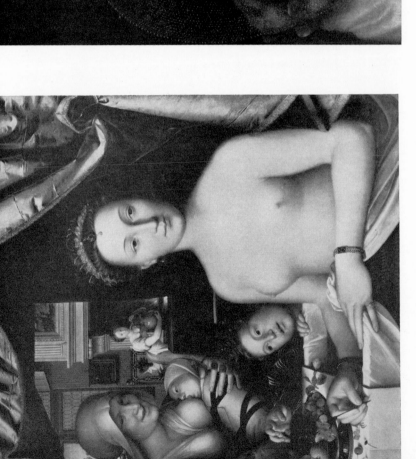

6 Portrait by François Clouet, generally thought to be that of Diane de Poiters, mistress of Henri II, but thought by some to be that of Marie Toucher, mistress of Charles IX.

(National Gallery of Art, Washington)

QUEEN MARGUERITE OF NAVARRE at the age of seventeen, by François Clouet.

blow that Charles, who was obviously taken unawares, was completely stunned:

'I desire to speak to you as a trusty servant,' he said, 'because I cannot conceal from you the danger you are in if you persist in your determination to do justice to M. de Guise. For you must know that the attempt on the Admiral's life has been planned, not only by M. de Guise, but also by your brother and your mother.'

Charles was stupefied. Was he going to have one of these quasi-demented reactions which the Italian knew so well? To avoid such a crisis, Gondi went on talking. He justified Catherine's action, portrayed her as anxious only for her son's and the State's well-being, reminded the King of the Catholics' hostility to intervention in the Netherlands, and showed how the Queen Mother was anxious at the thought of a new civil war in which the King risked being rejected by both parties. Gondi then complained of Maurevert's clumsiness, yet the King still showed no response. Gondi went on to speak of the Tuileries decision, although he was careful to present them as the conclusions of a council held without the King's presence.

Charles was perhaps not yet convinced, but he no longer spoke of arresting Henri de Guise or bringing him to justice. He remained silent, frowning, and the Florentine played for time, trying to avoid silence between them while he awaited the moment for Catherine to enter.

Presently she came in with Anjou at her heels. Even before her Florentine accomplice had made the merest gesture to warn her, she understood the situation, for she knew her son well and had detected at once the anger in his looks. Into the King's presence she brought the councillors who had attended her during the afternoon, together with Morvillier, who was Keeper of the Seals after L'Hôpital and before Birague. They all approached the King and his mother, so that the discussion could continue without raised voices.

The Queen spoke and her arguments were very different from Gondi's. She began by revealing a Huguenot conspiracy:

'The Huguenot party is taking arms against you. The Admiral has sent several despatches to Germany to raise 10,000 cavalry and to the Swiss Cantons to raise the same number of infantry. Throughout the kingdom the Huguenot captains are recruiting troops. They have appointed the day and the place for the rendezvous. Their foreign allies are to join them.

Weak as you are in men and money, you are not secure in any part of your kingdom.'

'Proofs!' demanded Charles.

'Bouchavannes, Piles, Pardaillan,' answered the Queen, calling as witnesses those who had heard Bouchavannes' report or been present at the King's supper.

As Charles still seemed sceptical, Catherine played her last card:

'You must know that the Catholics, weary of such endless troubles and dreading new disasters, are resolved to make an end of them. If the King does not take their advice—that is, strike first by killing the Huguenot leaders tonight—they are determined to elect a captain-general and organize a league under his leadership. Thus you will be left alone, powerless and without authority, exposed to the worst dangers. France will be torn between two big parties, over which you will have no command and from which you will get no obedience.'

Faced with this very precise threat the King wavered. The Queen had said enough and she simply added:

'Just one thrust of the sword tonight, and you can crush a terrible danger which threatens you and the State, prevent endless ruin and the murder of thousands.'

She had won.

Gondi had already shaken the King, but she had struck home. Charles well knew that the captain-general she was alluding to would be his own brother of whom he was jealous and whom he hated.

It was quite possible that he did not believe the whole story, and he still had grave doubts about the Huguenot plot. No matter! If there was no other way to prevent Anjou, supported by the Queen, from triumphing over him, the King would believe in it, like the rest. One by one his councillors agreed. Anjou, according to his own story, added a few more arguments, and the others 'forgot nothing which might serve to convince the King'. According to *l'Homme de Qualité et d'Honneur* who published Anjou's alleged confession much later, Gondi was the only one to let them down when his turn came to give advice, and the opinion he voiced was quite contrary to that of the Queen and the other councillors. Is it likely? It seems more logical to think that the *Discours* attributed to the future Henry III had been 'organized' in the interest of Retz and his descendants. The document has been questioned often, sometimes violently, by scholars who have come to contradictory conclusions, some rejecting it and others regarding it as wholly valid. It seems that in the present circumstances one may take it into consideration but with great care and only partially. It is unlikely that Anjou, when he was the King of Poland, should have dictated that account, as it now stands, to his physician Miron, as was long believed. It is more probable that it was reconstituted from authentic elements—oral or written—originating with Anjou. Such has been the conclusion of Jean L'Héritier,[1] who wrote of the *Discours*: 'It has certainly been fabricated, but it has not been invented, except as concerns the part given to Gondi, which is in complete disagreement with all the reliable sources.'

On the other hand, one feels inclined to believe the other Florentine, Cavriana,[2] though he was not present at the council, when he wrote that Morvillier remained speechless when his turn came to utter an opinion. After which he stammered: 'It is of great moment and requires careful thought. . . .' We must remember that Morvillier was the one man who had not taken part in the secret meeting at the Tuileries, which is enough to account for his bewilderment.

However, even with one discordant voice, the plot had been well set and it worked well. The King's fury might have provoked the ruin of Catherine and Anjou; yet, with the most horrible blasphemies, it had now turned against the Protestants.

All through his wretched life Charles had pursued innumerable stags and deer to death; now he was, in his own turn, the creature at bay. For two hours his shattered nerves had undergone the worst strain. His mother, his brother, his counsellors surrounded him, hemmed him in and harassed him, all pitilessly weighing upon the springs which could release his homicidal rage. He suddenly stood up, unable to utter anything but hideous screams, as if it were necessary at last to hear his own voice:

'God's death! Kill them! Kill them all, so that none may come back to blame me! Go! Give the order quickly!'

And he rushed madly to the door and retired to his own room, leaving them in his study.

[1] Héritier: *Catherine de Medicis*.
[2] Letter from Cavriana to Francisco de' Medici, August 26th.

The King's 'sudden and marvellous metamorphosis'—as his brother described it—enabled them to act, and at great speed. In order to have this mass execution carried out in a somewhat legal fashion, it was necessary to have the King's actual order to take such extraordinary measures against some of his subjects. They had got it and they felt relieved, including the Keeper of the Seals. The words, torn at last from the King, gave legal authority to what otherwise would have been a mere plot or conspiracy.

Here was no better irony: it is Tavannes who tells us that a King 'has more right to act in an extraordinary way against his subjects than they have to act against him'. The royal family and their councillors were now making use of the fictitious Huguenot plot of their own making to call up the city militia.

Catherine at once ended a debate which could only matter to lawyers. Now that the decision to kill had been taken—and to kill that very night—there was no time to be wasted: a list of victims had to be made and the killers designated. Briefly, the slaughter had to be organized properly and methodically.

'Kill them all!' the King had shouted, who by that time was probably in a hysterical state alone in his room. Catherine had not asked for so much, and above all, she did not wish to find herself the next day, when the 'King's justice' had been done, face to face with the Guises. It was necessary to examine the names of the various leaders one by one and to see which lives could be spared so that, after the crisis, the see-saw game could be played again. However, to gain time the Council ended with an almost superfluous question: Coligny, his son-in-law and all the Huguenots who had been gathered in the Rue de Béthisy trap must die. So that the Admiral would not escape this time, he had only to be left to the young Guise.

'Fetch the Duke,' ordered Catherine.

In the King's name, M. de Losse went to the Guises' palace and summoned the Duke, asking him to come to the Louvre at once. Meanwhile, they were quickly running over a number of marginal cases. For instance, there was a Huguenot house which should not only be spared, but specially protected: a little dwelling with a lovely carved front, in a garden near the Rue Monceau-St-Gervais.[1] It was the house of Marie Touchet, the King's mistress. To please the King, Ambroise Paré,

[1] Now Rue François-Miron.

his surgeon, was also to be spared, even if found at the Admiral's bedside. A worthy daughter of the Medicis, Catherine decided to save one life, that of Bernard Palissy, for whom she had set up a workshop and an oven in the Tuileries itself. It was lucky for him that he had not finished modelling and baking all the richly coloured ceramics the Queen had ordered.[1]

These 'details' having been settled without difficulty the main point in the deliberations was reached. The names that came under discussion were those of men belonging to the only two houses which could challenge the Lorraine princes' supremacy in France: Bourbon and Montmorency. It is here, moreover, that contemporary documents disagree widely. The obvious reason is that most of the accounts written by people who attended the fateful council meeting were not published until long afterwards, when the King was not a Valois but Henri de Bourbon himself who, after several campaigns and a change of religion, had become King of France and Navarre. For the same reason, the *Discours* which is ascribed to Anjou has been tampered with, or wholly written, to please the Gondis. As for Tavannes' *Mémoires*, copied and published by one of his sons, they betray the editor's secret, with touching clumsiness, through this guileless sentence: 'It was thanks only to the voice of M. de Tavannes that the lives of the present king, that great Henri IV, and the late Prince de Condé were spared. . . . It is most painful for M. de Tavannes' descendants that Henri de Navarre did not hear of it.' This shows why Tavannes' evidence is not to be relied on too much; yet it deserved to be quoted, if only because no other witness gives an equally detailed account of the discussion during which Henri's fate was in the balance.

If Tavannes is to be believed, this is how he pleaded for the Bourbons and the Montmorencys:

'The young and innocent princes, Navarre and Condé,[2] must not suffer as if they were guilty. One may hope that, if they are well taught and surrounded by servants duly selected by His Majesty, they may be brought back to the Catholic religion and to obedience to the King, their cousin. As for the Montmorencys, if they have favoured the Huguenots, they are not convicted of treason. To kill them would be to extinguish a house, one that can stand up to the Guises.'

[1] Nevertheless, he died in prison for his faith a few years later.
[2] Navarre was nineteen, and Condé, his cousin, twenty.

And if one can still believe Tavannes, this is how Retz replied:

'I completely disagree. All must be killed. Those young princes, who have been brought up in the reformed faith, cruelly hurt by the death of their uncle and friends,[1] will bitterly resent that loss and there will be no lack of men to incite them to vengence. One cannot transgress by halves. Remember Brutus: according to him, Caesar was the one culprit and he spared Mark Anthony's life, so that the latter got the people to rebel against him and brought about his downfall. In such extraordinary circumstances, one has to decide first what is expedient and justified, and act accordingly, so that nothing can distract one from one's aim. If laws are violated, they must be violated to the utmost, for the sin is the same, whether much or little has been attempted.'

Not content with reporting Retz's intervention thus, Tavannes implied that the Florentine would not have spoken in such terms except to make the positions of Marshal of France vacant in the hope that he might be chosen to replace one of them. It is obvious that Tavannes and Retz—or their descendants—had sought to ingratiate themselves with the Bourbons, and there is no doubt that the Duke de Nevers did all he could to save Condé, who had become his brother-in-law a few days earlier when marrying the lovely Marie de Clèves.[2] On the other hand, there is no question that Anjou, for the same reason, would rather have saved all the other Huguenot leaders but Condé: he was so much in love with Marie that he always wore 'her portrait round his neck in the form of a medallion'.[3] Yet the one who led the game was Catherine, and she was not interested in her son's unlucky love affair, or in Gondi's thwarted ambition. He wanted to preserve a few heads to be able to play them against the Lorraine princes. Navarre was her son-in-law, Condé and the Montmorencys were indispensable to her politics. All the others could perish, including the charming La Rochefoucauld, though he was related to the Bourbons and the King loved him dearly.[4]

[1] Coligny was Condé's great uncle: the young man's mother, Eleanore de Roye, was the Admiral's niece. His connection with Henri de Navarre was more distant: Antoine de Bourbon was the princess of Condé's brother-in-law.

[2] They had married in July 1572. She was beautiful, cultured and a staunch Protestant, though she certainly flirted with Anjou. She died in 1574.

[3] Pierre de L'Estoile, *op. cit.*

[4] His wife and Eleanore de Roye were sisters.

Meanwhile, a newcomer was ushered in: Henri de Guise, on whom they reckoned to carry out the essential task, and who, that very morning, had been almost driven from the Louvre by the King, but whom Losse had just gone to find on the King's orders. Guise already knew what was expected of him and was savouring his revenge in advance. One could be sure that he would not rely that night on a mere Maurevert and a single arquebuse. While discussing with Tavannes (who had been put in charge of the military operations, because he was, so to speak, the most senior of those of highest rank), the means placed at his disposal, the Provost of the Merchants had been fetched from the City Hall: Le Charron, and, because he was more reliable, his predecessor Marcel, who for a year had occupied the lucrative functions of Receiver-General of the Clergy.

Guise was to be responsible for Coligny, Téligny and the Protestant party in the Rue dé Béthisy. With him he was to have his uncle Aumale and the King's bastard brother, the young Chevalier d'Angoulême. The latter was most desirous to ensure Coligny's murder, as he was hoping to acquire the rank of Admiral of France, which would then fall vacant. In order to carry out the raid on Coligny's lodgings, Guise was to take his own men and Cosseins' fifty arquebusiers, who were on the spot to protect the Admiral. Other troops were gathered in the courtyard of the Louvre, since the Huguenots in the King of Navarre's retinue who were staying in the Palace had also to be dealt with. Charles IX had come back into the room and he was now listening intently to the preparations. He was going to take command of the garrison in the Louvre: after all, as King he was chief of the armies. He was now issuing orders: his 1,200 guards and the Catholic Swiss guards were to be summoned at once.

The city magistrates

It was the King who received the Provost Le Charron and his predecessor Marcel and explained what they were expected to do. The scene has been briefly related by all the witnesses in almost identical terms, but there are two more detailed accounts which supplement each other without contradiction. One was entered in the city register of Paris; the other was penned by a contemporary who obviously was not a witness of the scene he describes, but who could have been directly and minutely informed; this was Giovanni Michieli, the Venetian Envoy Extraordinary in Paris.

Here are the essential parts written by the city secretary under Le Charron's dictation, as soon as the latter had returned to the City Hall:

'Today, Saturday, August 23, 1572, President Le Charron, the Provost of the Merchants, has been summoned by the King to the Palace of the Louvre very late at night, and the King's Majesty declared to the said Provost in the presence of the Queen his mother and Monseigneur the Duke of Anjou his brother, and other princes and noble lords, that he had been warned that those of the new religion were seeking to rise by conspiracy against His Majesty and his State, and disturb the peace of his subjects and his city of Paris.'

The King having mentioned 'some haughty words, ringing with threats', which the Huguenots had uttered in his presence, he then enjoined and 'ordered the Provost to seize the keys of all the city gates and have them carefully locked; to have all the boats brought to the city bank and chained there; to have weapons delivered to captains, lieutenants, ensigns and burghers able to use them, and have them in readiness at each crossroad, to receive and carry out the King's orders; to have the city artillery ready both in the City Hall and in the Place de Grève'.[1]

The city registers also mention orders dispatched to various officers to broadcast the news. As for Giovanni Michieli, who may have been influenced by some recollection of the Commedia dell'Arte, he slipped into the very serious report he sent to the Most Serene Republic the rough draft of a very entertaining dialogue. According to him—and he may be right—the main character was not Le Charron but rather Claude Marcel, his predecessor, a small jeweller of the Pont-au-Change who had succeeded through great cunning and complete lack of honesty in rising to the top rank in the City Council.

'The King, won over by his mother and brother, summoned the Provost of the Merchants of Paris, a man called Marcel, a man of action and completely devoted to the Louvre. He was asked how many men the King could rely on, were he in need of

[1] Now Place de l'Hôtel de Ville.

the men of Paris. Marcel replied that it depended on how long notice he would have.

' "In a month?" he was asked.

'He answered: "More than 100,000; really any number the King may need."

' "And were they required within a week?" the Queen added.

' "It would be in proportion with 100,000 in a month," the Provost answered.

' "And were it within a day?"

' "More than 20,000."

'He was sworn to strict secrecy and silence. He was ordered to warn the district chiefs that very night, to be at home, ready with weapons and lights in their hands, and likewise sworn to secrecy. The order was carried out with such care and secrecy that no one knew what the other was doing. No one could make out what was the matter, and they were all the more watchful.'[1]

Le Charron and Marcel had also been given secret instructions which they were to pass on to the troops only at the last minute. The signal would be given at dawn by the bell of the Palace clock which was to start ringing the alarm, followed by all the church bells: lighted torches should then be placed at every window. Burghers and soldiers were to tie white shirt sleeves to their left arms and white crosses to their hats to distinguish themselves from Huguenots who would attempt to flee.

The last question was: how to recognize all the lodgings occupied by Huguenots? Claude Marcel at once reassured the King and all the others: he had seen to this in the afternoon with his officers, by marking every house with a cross. Obviously, he had supervised the operation when the Duke de Guise had gone out with Angoulême in Anjou's coach.

The vigil

The Council was over and its members now went ostensibly to bed, so as not to arouse the Huguenots' suspicion. Catherine was the first to retire to her apartments, probably because she was the most intent to dismiss her attendants and get up again. The young Queen Marguerite of Navarre has left a vivid and precise account of the scene:

'In the evening, I went to the Queen my Mother, when she was about to go to bed. I was sitting on a chest next to my sister

[1] Quoted by M. Baschet in *Les princes de l'Europe au XVIe siècle*.

of Lorraine, who was looking very sad. The Queen was talking to someone else, then she turned round and told me to go to bed. As I was curtseying, my sister grabbed my arm and stopped me and, bursting into tears, said: "In God's name, sister, do not go!" And I was greatly alarmed.

'The Queen my mother noticed it and, calling to my sister, got very angry and forbade her to tell me anything. My sister said that it was a shame to send me to be sacrified like that, and that undoubtedly, if they noticed something, they would revenge themselves on me. The Queen answered that, if it pleased God, no evil would befall me, but whatever happened I had to go, otherwise it would look suspicious . . . and again she ordered me to bed, very harshly. My sister was in tears and she bade me goodnight, not daring to say more, and I went, greatly frightened and dismayed, and unable to imagine what I had to fear.'

While that scene was taking place in Catherine's apartment, the King was going to bed with the usual ceremony: an incident took place, which was hardly noticed but was recorded by Tavannes. A quarrel broke out between the fiery Pardaillan and Nambur, the King's usher at the door of the Royal apartment. Undoubtedly because of Pardaillan's insolent attitude at supper, Nambur tried to forbid him to enter the room and they almost came to blows.

When all the courtiers but one had gone, another episode took place and it is mentioned by a first-hand authority, as Mergey saw and heard everything:

'The Comte de la Rochefoucauld, as usual, was the last to stay with the King; we were waiting for him, Chamont and I, in the next room. Hearing the tapping of shoes, as when someone bows, I drew near to the door and I heard the King say to the Count:

' "Foucauld" (he always called him that), "don't go; it is late. We will gossip for the rest of the night."

' "That is impossible," he answered; "you must go to bed and sleep."

' "You can sleep with my valets," said the King.

' "No, their feet stink," replied La Rochefoucauld. "Goodnight, my little master."

'And he went to spend an hour with the Dowager Princess Condé, to whom he made love.'[1]

[1] Mergey, *Mémoires*.

Thus, at the last minute Charles IX had tried to give his friend 'Foucauld' a chance to escape the massacre. But his friendship did not go so far as to warn him of the danger that threatened him if he left the one inviolate sanctuary, the King's bedroom.

It was quite a different atmosphere in Henri de Navarre's apartment; more like a guard room than the bedroom of a king who had been married for six days to the loveliest princess in Paris. The latter, who had just left the Queen Mother's apartments 'in great fright and dismay', not knowing what she had to fear, went back to her own closet to pray to God 'to take me under His protection and to protect me against I knew not what. Then the King my husband, who had gone to bed, sent word to me to join him, which I did. I found his bed surrounded by thirty or forty Huguenots whom I did not know. They did nothing but talk all through the night'.

Mergey also tells how little the intimacy of the newly married pair was respected that night, and he adds interesting details. It will be remembered that, after waiting for La Rochefoucauld in the King's outerchamber, he had escorted him to the door of the Dowager Princess of Condé.

'From there he went to the King of Navarre's room, and having wished him goodnight he withdrew in order to retire. At the foot of the staircase a man dressed all in black went up to him and, taking him aside, talked to him for a long time. The Count de La Rochefoucauld then called me and told me to go back to the King of Navarre's room to let him know that he had just been warned that M. de Guise and M. de Nevers were in town and would not sleep in the Louvre.

'I found the King in bed with the Queen his wife, and having whispered into his ear the Count's message, he asked me to beg him to come first thing in the morning, as he had promised.

'Returning to the Count, I saw him at the foot of the staircase with M. de Nançay, the captain of the guard: I did not deliver my message in front of the latter, but the Count and M. de Nançay went back to the King of Navarre's room, where they entered without me and stayed a long time.'

Mergey's account does not stop there. Its author showed a great gift of observation. He went on to relate an incident of which he was the witness while in Navarre's apartments, where the thirty or forty Huguenot lords were assembled, the men mentioned by Queen Marguerite. They had gone into a dressing-room with only an arras to separate them from the main room. 'M. de Nançay,' wrote Mergey, 'pulled up the tapestry and putting his head into the dressing-room, saw that it was more or less full, some playing cards, others chatting. He spent some time counting them and shaking his head, and then said: "Gentlemen, if any of you want to leave, I warn you that the gates are about to be closed". But they answered that they meant to spend the night there, as they were keen to go on playing. Upon which the Count and M. de Nançay went down into the courtyard where all the guard companies were arrayed, Swiss, Scotsmen and French.'

Mergey adds that when La Rouchefoucauld, Chamont and himself left the Louvre, M. de Rambouillet, with whom he had been a prisoner in Flanders, said to him in a most doleful voice, as he opened the gate he was guarding: 'Goodbye, M. de Mergey, my dear friend!' However surprising it may be, it seems that neither La Rochefoucauld nor Mergey suspected anything, not even after they had seen this unaccountable assembly of troops in the courtyard at dead of night.

They left and went quietly to bed on the mattresses which had been laid out for them in improvised lodgings near Coligny's house.

Everything was peaceful and silent in the Rue de Bethisy where Cossein's men were mounting guard, and in the lower courtyard of the Admiral's house where Navarre's five Swiss were also on the watch. A light was still burning in Coligny's room, but only a few people were sitting round the wounded man. Téligny and his young wife, Louise de Coligny, had already returned to their quarters in a neighbouring house. Apart from the Admiral's servants, there were with him only Nicolas Muss, his interpreter,[1] Belon his secretary, his surgeons, Ambroise Paré and Thomas, a few friends, a student, Salomon Certon, the Pastor Pierre Merlin,[2] the comptroller Bruneau, and

[1] A young German. He stayed with Coligny to the end and was killed with him.

[2] He had been sent to Coligny by the Genevese authorities and was one of the very last to leave him. When escaping over the roof, he fell into a garret and remained hidden there for several days. A hen, apparently living in the garret, laid an egg each day into his hand, enabling him to survive. He managed to escape from Paris and attached himself to the Admiral's children, whom he followed to Switzerland and then back to France. Later, he went to England and died in 1603.

two noblemen, Pierre de la Gillière, Seigneur de Cornaton, and Pierre de Malras, Baron de Yolet.[1]

It was midnight. A citizen of Strasbourg, who was staying in Paris for a short time, crossed the Louvre district at that hour. Later, when back in his native city, he was to bear evidence 'that he had been able to go home quietly and without trouble'.[2]

---

[1] He managed to escape from Paris the next day. He fought at La Rochelle, held various high military appointments under Henri de Navarre and was a member of his sister's retinue. He died in 1614.

[2] The document was found in the Palatin Elector's archives and translated by R. Reuss (*Bulletin de la société d'histoire du protestantisme français*, T. XXII, p. 377).

CHAPTER THREE

The Blood-Soaked Morning

Two o'clock in the morning of August 24th, the day of St Bartholomew, apostle and martyr.

The King, the Queen Mother and Anjou rose and dressed, having retired and pretended to go to bed for an hour or two. They met in one of the rooms on the ground floor which overlooked the courtyard, and through the open window they watched and listened. The night was stifflingly hot and a few lights were glimmering here and there. Harsh voices were bawling orders, and the clatter of weapons and armour could be heard as Swiss, Scottish and Gascon guards assembled. Suddenly there were shouts. The words could not be distinguished but it was easy to realize that people were shouting abuse at one another and possibly coming to blows. Then a musket shot, very close and loud, rang through the night.

Can we believe Anjou, who wrote, long after the event: 'We could not tell where it had been fired or if anyone had been hurt, but I remember well that we were deeply impressed by the sound, both in our senses and in our minds, seized with terror and dread at the thought of the great disorders that were about to take place'?

He did not confine himself simply to the terror and dread aroused by a single pistol shot, which would have been rather surprising after a whole day devoted to the planning of wholesale slaughter. He added: 'To prevent it, we sent one of our attendants in haste to M. de Guise to order him most urgently to return to his house and to take care to do nothing to the Admiral; this order alone would stop everything, since it had been decided that nothing was to take place anywhere in the city until the Admiral had been killed.'

Whether it was true—and the whole tale ascribed to the future Henri III is of doubtful accuracy—this belated decision cannot be credited to any last-moment qualm of conscience. The possible explanation is that the Queen Mother and her son, suddenly faced by a completely unexpected incident, realized that they were about to release forces which would later be very difficult to canalize and direct. The same meaning must be ascribed to what Tavannes wrote about Catherine who, according to him, would willingly have called the whole thing off.

What, then, had taken place under the Louvre windows, and who had fired the untimely shot?

The clattering armour, the shouting sergeants, and the movement of troops, which had been overheard by Catherine and her son, had also disturbed people who had every possible reason not to sleep too soundly. A few Huguenot noblemen, living near Coligny's residence, had been awakened by the turmoil and were worried. They dressed hurriedly and went out to see what was afoot. Seeing assembled troops, doubled outposts and piled arms, they had shown greater perspicacity than La Rochefoucauld. They haughtily demanded an explanation. Insults were exchanged and some Gascon guards, threatened with violence by a few Huguenots, charged at them with their pikes. Soon they were all involved in a skirmish and the guards, realizing that if one of the Protestants escaped alive he would raise the alarm at once, prepared to kill them to the last man. The pistol shot was probably fired at one who was running away.

Even if the Queen and her son had really wished to desist, it was already too late: blood had already been shed. Besides, according to Anjou, they saw at once how pointless it was to hesitate. A moment later, the gentleman who had been sent to Guise returned; 'He told us that M. de Guise had replied that it was too late, that the Admiral was dead and that things were starting all over the city. We then went back to our first plan and shortly afterwards allowed things to take their course.'

They did not even remain passive, according to authoritative evidence. Far from allowing matters to take their own course, Catherine meant to keep control of them. To begin with, she did not wait until the Law Courts bell rang at the agreed hour, an hour and a half later. She ordered the tocsin to be sounded at once. She ordered the big bell of St Germain l'Auxerrois to be tolled, the Marie, which was cast in 1525 and had never been rung except for royal masses.

Soon other bells clanged in answer, torches flared in the windows and shots were fired all over the city, and even in the Louvre, drowning the first screams of the victims. In a few minutes the King, without leaving his balcony, could witness in his own palace a scene worthy of one of Nero's orgies.

The Guises' revenge

Henri de Guise could not wait for the signal before rushing to the Rue de Béthisy. From the moment when he was ordered by the King himself to murder Coligny, he was out of control. Giovanni Michieli had noticed his restlessness and written: 'Your Serene Highness can easily imagine the pleasure with which M. de Guise received the order and the enthusiasm with which he carried it out . . .'

Guise arrived at the Admiral's house with a large escort. Did it really number 300 officers and men, as some witnesses said, or just sixty horsemen and a few soldiers, according to others? It does not matter much, for all are agreed as to which among Guise's companions took the leading parts.

The Duke was on horseback like those who were with him. The flaring torches enabled people to recognize some of the men who clattered up to the Rue de Béthisy: Aumale and Angoulème, and some ten or twelve gentlemen of less importance, all of them followers of the house of Lorraine: Nicolas de Halwin, Edmé d'Hautefort, the Baron de Cessac, Raymond de Cardaillac (Seigneur de Sarlabous, who has often been confused with his brother Corbeyran de Cardaillac, Governor of Le Havre), Jean de Biran and three foreigners—the notorious Pietro-Paolo Tosinghi, who was first regarded as the incompetent gunman who fired at Coligny, Achille Petruzzi from Sienna (one of Francis de Guise's former equeries) and Jean Yanowitz, nick-named Besme (short for 'Bohême', on account of his Czech origin), all very obscure persons.

When they reined in at Coligny's house, an officer came to meet them: this was Cosseins, who was to admit the murderers into the house he had been sent to protect. He went to the door and called for Coligny's housekeeper, Labonne, who had the keys.

'Open, in the King's name! I must see your master at once.'

Labonne suspected nothing; he opened the door and was stabbed to death at once, falling without time to utter a warning shout. But the King of Navarre's five Protestant Swiss had followed him into the courtyard and, though one of them was shot almost at point blank, the rest ran back into the house and barred the door, while the Admiral's servants came down and helped them to pile furniture behind it, hoping to halt the murderers.

On the first floor, in the wounded man's room, Muss, Cornaton, Ambroise Paré and Thomas were gathered around the Admiral who, though very weak, had got out of bed and was putting on his dressing gown. He requested Pastor Merlin to say a prayer. Coligny still believed in the King's word, and he asked Muss to open the window and call for help. Cosseins would come, since he was responsible for his safety! Muss saw at once the white doublets of the cavalry and the Swiss of the King's guard, and realized that no help could be expected from that quarter.

'What means this disturbance?' asked Paré in dismay.

Salomon Certon[1] had just carried down a chest to help strengthen the barricade, and had seen the Guise men breaking through the first door. He turned to Coligny:

'My Lord, God is summoning us to Him; we cannot hold out.'

'I have been ready to die for a long time,' answered the Admiral. 'All of you must try to escape if it is possible, for you cannot save my life ... I commend my soul to the mercy of God.'

They obeyed his last order—all except Nicolas Muss, who would not abandon his master—and they went up to the garret, got on to the roof through a window and then over to the next house, slipping away into the darkness.

Meanwhile, on the ground floor the men who had been trying to defend the staircase were overwhelmed; the second door was burst open and Anjou's Swiss guards—recognizable by the black, white and green of their uniforms—rushed into the vestibule. Seeing their Protestant countrymen, who were still defending the staircase, they hesitated a little, but Cosseins ordered his Gascon arquebusiers to shoot. One of Navarre's

[1] 1550-1614. Studied medicine and law, and wrote poetry. He took refuge in Geneva after the massacre, then came back to France to serve under Henri de Navarre. He translated the Odyssey into verse in 1604.

Swiss fell dead and the others were thrown down and trampled underfoot. Now nothing in the world could stop the murderers from entering Coligny's room, the door of which was not even barred.

Things happened very quickly now, so quickly that it is impossible to check the various versions of the story, though they often contradict one another. There is really nothing surprising in the fact that, when the actors of the drama wrote their accounts of it many years later, they gave various versions of the Admiral's last words, or did not agree as to who entered or struck first.

Let us picture to ourselves the narrow staircase, reeking with powder smoke, up which people who had scarcely known one another a moment before were racing: Swiss soldiers, Cosseins, Sarlabous, Yanowitz. They were climbing up, shouting, wielding their swords, stepping over dead bodies and expecting a last show of resistance higher up. Suddenly they rushed into a dim and silent room, where they found a solitary man kneeling at the foot of his bed in prayer. They hated him, but nevertheless they could not avoid being impressed by his reputation and personality. Six or eight men, or more, broke into the room: it was fearfully overcrowded and they were all hampered by their weapons, their bucklers and their armour, shouting and banging into one another, gesticulating confusedly and brandishing their swords, their lances or their daggers. Later, they could not remember who said what, nor the abuse they shouted at their victim.

The names of the men who entered Coligny's room are known: they were Cosseins, Yanowitz, Sarlabous, de Halwin and four Swiss guards—Captain Joshua Studer von Winkelbach and three soldiers, Moritz Grünenfelder, Martin Koch and Conrad Bürg. One of the murderers, grabbing Coligny by the shoulder, dragged him into the light and snarled:

'Are you the Admiral, you rascal?'

The unhappy man had just time to assent, possibly adding, as some have said: 'Young man, you should respect my old age and infirmity, but you cannot shorten my life.' For the first blows had already fallen.

In the courtyard, Guise, Aumale and the bastard of Angoulême, who were above soiling their own hands with an executioner's work, were anxious to hear that all was over. Guise had sent his trusted Yanowitz with the gang and it was to him he shouted through an open window:

'Besme! Is it all over?'

'Yes, my lord.'

'Well, throw him out of the window. M. d'Angoulême won't believe it, if he doesn't see him at his feet.'

It seems that the Admiral was still breathing when they grabbed him. His hand or his foot caught in the window and one of the men thought he was still strong enough to resist, and shouted more abuse at him before tipping him over. Guise and his companions wanted to see their victim's face, and his blood had to be wiped away with a rag, revealing the well-known features.

'I recognize him; it is he,' said Guise.

According to some witnesses, he kicked the bloodstained face and then walked out of the courtyard to say to his men in the street:

'Well done! Be of good cheer! It has begun well. Now to the others, as the King orders.'

A few contemporaries—Brantôme, among them—refused to believe that Guise could be vile enough to kick the face of the man he had murdered. As if, for a man of noble birth, murder was less degrading than a kick in the victim's face! Faced with conflicting evidence one cannot be sure; yet, in such circumstances, at such a time, with a man as hot for revenge as Henri de Guise, such a gesture is far from unlikely.

On the other hand, all are agreed that Guise said nothing when one of his men—the Italian, Petruzzi—cut off Coligny's head with his dagger and carried it away, while his colleague Tosinghi searched the body and put Coligny's gold chain into his pocket.

Mass or death

Meanwhile the tocsin was sounding, and at the Louvre torches were spluttering at the windows as if for one of the torchlight balls of which the Court was so fond; inside the Palace the King was rousing himself to action, since he was in command in his own castle. He had stepped back from his balcony and ordered his brother-in-law and young Condé to be brought to him.

At the door of the King's apartment, the two young princes,

surrounded as usual by some of their retainers, among whom were Monneins and Piles, encountered guards in arms, who refused to let their companions in. Navarre understood at last. He turned and, with tears in his eyes, said sadly to his friends:

'Goodbye. God alone knows whether we shall meet again in this world.'

And the princes were led into the King's chamber. They were expecting to see him alone, but he was surrounded by Catherine, Anjou and the whole secret council. Navarre went up to Tavannes and asked the reason for this surprising meeting, but the Marshal confessed later that he did not dare to answer.

No one spoke but the King, and his first words made Condé and Navarre realize the extent of the slaughter:

'Having permitted so many civil wars to harm my kingdom,' shouted Charles, 'I have at last found means to prevent more trouble. I have ordered the Admiral to be killed, to pay for the many crimes of which he has been guilty. And all the rebellious heretics are to be dealt with in the same way. I well remember all the harm you two, as well as the Admiral, have done, but out of love for the Blood Royal of France that is in your veins, and out of pity for your youth, I will be so good as to forget the past. . . . But on one condition: you will atone for your sins by swearing fealty and obeissance to me, and by returning to our Mother, the Church of Rome. For I will have but one religion in my kingdom from now on: that of the kings who were on the throne before me. If you refuse to obey, speak at once, for you will receive the punishment that is being dealt out now to the other heretics, your accomplices.'

Henri de Navarre felt the ground reeling beneath his feet: he could not recognize in this demented monster the King who, a few hours earlier, was swearing to do justice to 'his father the Admiral'. Yet he knew he was to answer first. His inmost feelings were for yielding, for the present, to an adversary who was now the stronger. His reply was very humble and he reminded the King of the closeness of their relationship and of the promises he had been given.

'I beg Your Majesty to consider that conscience is an important matter,' he said, 'and that it is very difficult to abandon the religion in which I have been brought up.'

Charles' eyes were blazing and Henri hastily added:

'Yet Your Majesty can be sure that I will do all I can to please him.'

Condé was more violent and less wary, and his faith was probably more ardent. He proved far less easy to manage. Indifferent to danger, he passionately replied:

'Sire, I remember that Your Majesty pledged his troth to me and to those of my religion so solemnly that I cannot believe that the King will commit perjury after such an oath. As for obeying the King, I always did and shall do so in the future, without fail. But, as to my religion, if the King gave me leave to practise it, it was God who revealed it to me, and He is the one to whom I have to render account. Your Majesty has my body and my possessions in his power and can do with them as he pleases, but I have decided to remain firm in my faith, which I take as the one true faith, even if I die for it.'

Mad with rage, Charles IX was scarcely able to remain silent while the young man was speaking. He had scarcely finished when Charles burst out:

'You rebel and son of a rebel! So, this is how you repay me for having spared your life, while you should have died with the other heretics! I give you three days to change your mind and be instructed in the Roman faith. Three days! And, God's death, I will not hesitate to have your head chopped off if you have not changed your mind! Three days, and then you choose between the mass or death! Meanwhile, have them both locked into my apartment and summon Nançay. He shall answer for them with his life!'

Under the King's eyes

Claude de la Châtre, Seigneur de Nançay, Captain of the Guards, shouldered a heavy burden during that frightful night in the Palace, where everybody had been suddenly awakened and the massacre was about to begin. The Huguenots in Navarre's and Condé's retinue, whom the King himself had ordered to sleep near their masters to protect them from Guise's enterprises, were led by Nançay and his guards into one of the wings of the castle, together with their servants, tutors and secretaries, and had their weapons taken from them, when the princes were brought into the King's presence. Now everyone was waiting for the King to return to his balcony so that the 'merry-making' might begin. At last he came to his window, attended by his mother and his brother. The Swiss, who had been generously plied with wine, had been placed, on M. d'O's orders, two abreast in front of the gate leading into the court-yard. Then Nançay and his men drove the Protestant lords towards the gate and, as soon as they were past it, they were struck down with every kind of weapon, halberds, lances and clubs, and despatched with swords or daggers. Among the first to fall were Ségur, Baron de Pardaillan, Louis Goulard de Beauvois, and Pont-Breton. A few of them managed to speak to their murderers before falling, including St Martin, called Brichanteau, a charming young man who had been much loved and admired at Court for bearing and wisdom beyond his years. Seeing the Swiss captain about to strike him, the boy, who was more surprised than frightened, staggered him with a candid question:

'Alas! what have I done?'

But the murderer did not hesitate for long and, plunging his sword into the young man's body, answered with a sneer:

'Then be comforted if you have done nothing, and die innocent!'

Another victim held out for a while against the yelling pack of killers: he was one of the bravest men of his time, and they all knew him. He was Captain de Piles, of whom it was said that he used to wear a necklace made of priests' ears. At St Jean d'Angély he had been taken prisoner by the King in person and, according to the sacred laws of chivalry, the latter was respon-sible for his safety. Piles saw the King standing at his balcony and, shouting himself hoarse, called to him, challenged him and abused him. Charles remained silent. Then Piles, turning round, took off his beautiful cloak and handed it to one of the King's officers, saying:

'Take it, Sir. Piles gives it to you. Keep it and always re-member the death of a man so shamefully murdered.'

But the officer was terrified, realizing that everybody was watching him, and he did not dare to accept the cloak, lest he might have to follow Piles in death. He turned away. Meanwhile, one of his men despatched the Huguenot with his halberd and there was one more body to cast on top of the rest.

In the Palace a few Huguenots who had succeeded in slipping through Nançay's fingers were racing through tortuous pas-sages, hoping to find a refuge and save their lives. Henri's room was now silent, as he and his companions had left. Queen Marguerite had drawn the bed curtains and, completely exhausted, had succeeded in falling asleep. She did not hear the clanging bells or the screams echoing in the passages, or the racing feet. Suddenly someone banged on the door with feet and fists and she woke with a start. An anxious voice was shouting: 'Navarre! Navarre!' Terrified, and thinking it might be Marguerite's husband, her nurse opened the door:

'It was M. de Téjan,'[1] the Queen wrote later. 'He had been wounded in the arm and the elbow, and four archers were after him and rushed with him into the room. To escape, he threw himself on my bed. Feeling that man grabbing me, I slipped between the bed and the wall, and he slipped after me, still grasping me tightly. I did not know him and did not know whether he was there to insult me, or whether the archers were after him or after me. We were both screaming and equally frightened. Then, thank God, M. de Nançay entered, and seeing me in such a state he could not refrain from laughing, though he felt moved and, getting angry, sent the archers away, upbraiding them for their lack of courtesy, and he made me a present of the life of the poor man who was still embracing me. I had him attended to and his wounds dressed, and he was put to bed in my closet until he was quite well. While I was changing my shift, as it was soaked with blood, M. de Nançay told me what was taking place and that my husband was in the King's chamber and would come to no harm. He made me put on a cloak and took me to Mme de Lorraine's (my sister's) room, and I arrived there more dead than alive.

'When I came into the vestibule, all the doors of which were open, I saw a gentleman named Bourse running for dear life, with archers in pursuit, and they pierced him with their halberds within three paces from me. I almost fainted into M. de Nancay's arms, thinking that we had both been pierced by the same stroke. When I had recovered a little, I entered my sister's little bedroom. While I was there, M. de Miossens,[2] first gentleman to the King, my husband, and Armagnac, his first valet, came to me to beg for their lives. I went and threw myself at the feet of the King

[1] In fact, the man was Gaston de Lévis, Viscount de Léran. He escaped the massacre but was killed the same year, fighting with the Protestants. He had married Gabrielle de Foix and had been a staunch follower of Henry of Navarre.

[2] He remained one of Henri IV's staunchest followers.

87

and Queen to beg for them, and they finally granted me their lives.'

Her tale is not lacking in colour; it is obvious that she did, saw and felt all she wrote. Thanks to her, three men were saved. So were a few others: Gramont, Gamache, Duras and, of course, Bouchavannes! For other reasons, and their contemporaries are quite candid about it: 'They were forgiven all the more easily as the King well knew that they had little or no religion'.

On the other hand, Charles IX had not turned a hair while Piles was appealing as a gentleman to his loyalty, and he proved merciless when appeals were made to him to save, not non-entities or men of no religion, but some of Coligny's trusted followers. He showed no pity towards La Rochefoucauld, Téligny or Monneins; the latter was in the courtyard with Fervaque, one of the officers who was to kill him and who was still trying to protect him with his body. Fervaque, leaving Monneins to trusted men, went and threw himself at the King's feet. He had faithfully served the Catholic cause and from Picardy had just brought fifty horsemen very hostile to the Huguenots. He was not asking for a favour. He begged the King, as a reward for past services, to grant him the life of Monneins, his oldest and dearest friend. Charles listened impatiently and pronounced the verdict:

'God's death! Out of consideration for what you have done for me, I will forget that you begged for that devil's life! But I order you to kill him with your own hands.'

Fervaque actually disobeyed the King; that is, he left others to murder Monneins, but did not go so far as to save his life.

Between men of quality

As the signal had been given earlier than was ordered, the Parisians, roused by Marcel and Le Charron, did not see the first act of the drama. They arrived only in the early morning. By that time the Swiss had slaughtered all the King's guests in the Louvre; the noblemen, who had been entrusted with special missions the night before, had already dispatched their allotted victims. The Valois court was ruled by a strict social hierarchy, even in such unprecedented circumstances, and it was agreed that noblemen were only to be murdered by their peers or, at the very lowest, by the King's guards.

Consequently, before dawn, while the burghers were still

assembling and getting ready, and while the last victims were being butchered in the Louvre, several horsemen were sent out by Guise, Aumale, Nevers and Montpensier to liquidate the last noblemen before the mob got in. Téligny could not be spared: he was the Admiral's son-in-law and also one of the cleverest of the party's advisers. He was living very near the Admiral. As soon as he heard the gang of murderers coming to his father-in-law's house he understood—too late—how right had been the Vidame de Chartres and his friends, who had refused to believe in the King's word of honour. He dressed in haste, ran up to the garret and got on to the roof, hoping to get away; but he was seen by one of Anjou's guards and shot down. His young wife, Louise de Coligny, was spared, though no one knows how she eventually escaped from Paris and later rejoined her brothers in Switzerland.[1]

The Baron de Soubise proved too rash: he lived near the Rue de Bethisy and, hearing the first shots, armed himself and ran to Coligny's assistance. Those who were after him had only to disarm him. They did not finish him off on the spot but dragged him to the Louvre, killed him and threw his body on top of the others. Guerchy, caught at home, fought hard. Alone against several men, his cloak rolled round his left arm, he was overwhelmed by numbers alone, but he killed two of his adversaries before he perished.

Now, in all the houses of the Rue de Béthisy, where most of the Protestant noblemen had been so conveniently collected, the killing proceeded, ten men to one. Some of the victims were massacred in bed, and some were cut down as, scantily clad, they tried to escape. That is how Puvieux, Baudiné (Acier-Berny's brother) and others died. Nor were their valets, pages and grooms spared. The King had concern only for the nobility and, in accordance with his orders, the corpses of Protestant captains and courtiers were dragged along the streets with ropes, like dead beasts, and thrown on to the gruesome heap in the Louvre.

The killers rushed into the Hôtel de Conti to kill Brion, the little marquess's tutor.[2] The old man thought they were after

---

[1] She was seventeen and had married Téligny in May 1571. Later, she married William the Silent as his fourth wife. Their only son, Frederick-Henry, was Statholder of the Netherlands after the death of Maurice, his half-brother.

[2] Antoine de Foucauld, Lord of Brion.

his pupil and took him in his arms to protect him, but the weeping child was wrenched from him, screaming to them to spare his tutor. It was of no avail and Brion was stabbed to death before the child's eyes. As for La Rochefoucauld, who had refused to sleep in the Louvre and had not even understood what was brewing when he saw the troops gathering, he was sound asleep in his primitive lodgings, possibly dreaming of the delightful time he had had with the Dowager Princesse de Condé. He was abruptly awakened by six masked men, who had broken into his room. He was used to the King's silly jokes and thought that they were masked dancers of some sort and that Charles was one of them.[1]

'Not so hard, my little master! Don't strike so hard!' he babbled pleasantly.

But the last word died in his throat: he had been stabbed by one of Anjou's valets, sent on purpose by his master. The others went on stabbing his corpse: among them were Captain Raymond, brother of Chicot, Anjou's jester, and La Barge, to whom La Rochefoucauld's company of men-at-arms had been promised. La Rochefoucauld's two companions, Mergey and Chamont, were luckier: there were too few mattresses in the house for them to stay, and they had found rooms in a nearby house. They managed to escape and Mergey told the story in his memoirs.

'We had scarcely gone to bed,' he wrote, 'when we heard the alarm and saw the Admiral's house attacked by the very men who had been sent by the King to protect him. I was well aware that things would not stop at that. I jumped out of bed and dressed as quickly as I could. Chamont was so thunderstruck that he stood there in his shirt, unable to think of anything. At last I got him dressed. When I was about to go out to find M. de la Rochefoucauld, Chamont said: "Why do you want us to go? We don't know who those people are. Let us wait a while". I took his advice and I was right, for had we gone into the street we would have been dispatched. Our room was part of a big house where the young Princesse de Condé's[2] retinue had been lodged. Hearing the great tumult and noise in the street,

---

[1] Francis III de la Rochefoucauld. He was converted to Protestantism after his second marriage to Condé's sister-in-law, Eleanor de Roye. When very young, he had fought in Metz in 1552. He was with Condé at Dreux and Jarnac, very much admired, respected and loved.

[2] Marie de Clèves, Louis de Condé's wife.

and people breaking in the doors, including those of the Admiral's house, I looked out of the window into the courtyard and saw two men standing there with bewildered expressions on their faces: they too were Huguenots and officers of the Princess. I recognized one of them and asked him to prop under our window a derelict stool which I saw on the ground, and I got out on to it, and then into the courtyard; so did Chamont. Meanwhile, after the Admiral had been killed in his room, thrown out of the window and identified by M. de Guise, the latter left with his party to attack the Huguenots round St Germain-des-Prés. I was still in the courtyard, near the gate, listening to what was happening. As the horsemen rode past, one of them asked: "Who lives here?" He said that it was the Princess's retinue, and he remarked: "That is not what we are after."'

From St Germain-des-Prés to Montfort l'Amaury

Hidden behind the gate of his courtyard, Mergey was eagerly listening: Guise and his men were clattering towards St Germain-des-Prés. The young man did not know that this ride was quite unexpected.

The night before, during the council held in the Louvre, Tavannes had organized three different operations to be carried out simultaneously against three different Protestant headquarters: the Louvre, the Rue de Béthisy and the Faubourg St Germain. The King and his brother were to settle the matter in the Louvre; Guise, Aumale and Angoulême undertook to liquidate the Rue de Béthisy; and Marcel and the city militia were to surround the Faubourg and see that no Huguenot escaped. The third operation was the most difficult by far: it required many men, as the houses occupied by Protestants on the left bank were much farther from one another than the apartments hastily commandeered round the Louvre. Marcel had arranged for about 1,000 men to go there, under Laurent de Maugiron, who had been put in command by the King. The commissar of the district and the comptroller Du Mas were to guide them to the Huguenot houses, which had also been marked with a white cross, as everywhere else in town.

The one man who questioned the efficiency of the organization was the Duc de Nevers. He remarked that, as the Faubourg was outside the city walls, a few Protestants might ride off after the first surprise and give warning. Consequently, he suggested sending a strong party of horsemen in advance to the Vaugirard gate to stop anyone from getting out. He offered to take command of that troop, as he was certain that this would prove a leading part. But the King and Queen refused to have one of their best councillors far away from them and possibly cut off from Paris if things did not turn out well. Nevers consequently was kept in the Louvre and his suggestion was dropped.

But his assumption was right and no one, the night before, could guess that the signal would be given two hours too soon. Thus, when the bells started ringing, Marcel's companies had not assembled, the Faubourg St Germain was not surrounded and Du Mas was still sound asleep.

It might not have been so bad if, as one might have assumed, the Huguenots in the Faubourg, cut off from the right bank of the Seine and with no boats to row them over, had been left in ignorance of what had happened in the Louvre and the Rue de Béthisy. The clanging bells might not have roused their suspicions, as they were used to noisy lauds and matins before dawn on the morning of great feasts, as was the case. But Providence sent a man to warn them and prevent them from being murdered in their beds. This man, 'who was neither seen nor heard of later', was a Protestant horsedealer. He had sold horses to a great Protestant nobleman, La Force from Périgord, who had come to Paris to attend Navarre's wedding, and he had felt a great and respectful sympathy for this high-ranking coreligionist.

The man had lodgings not far from the Rue de Béthisy and had witnessed the beginning of the massacre. He realized at once that La Force and his family were in the greatest danger, and he ran down to the river to cross it and warn him. All the barges were chained to the bank and he could not take one of them. He undressed at once—the water is warm in August—tied his clothes in a bundle on top of his head, swam the Seine and ran in haste to La Force's hostel, at the corner of the Rue de Seine and the Rue de Buci. He roused the whole house and related the 'terrible accident' which had befallen the Admiral and the Protestants on the other bank.

La Force did not hesitate for a second. He rushed to his brother's house in the Rue St Germain.[1] The latter sent his servants to summon the other Protestants, who came at once.

[1] Now Boulevard St Germain.

There was Montgomery, the Vidame de Chartres, Fontenay, of the house of Rohan, one of the Pardaillans, La Nocle and others. They did not waste time in talking. They all realized that every second was precious. They all agreed, not to run away and save their lives, as one might have expected, but to ride to the Louvre to save the King! For it did not occur to them for one second that Charles IX might be in league with the murderers, let alone that he might be their leader!

Scantily clad and armed in haste, they ran towards the Tour de Nesles,[1] where numerous barges were always chained. When they arrived, they were greatly surprised: there was not a boat in sight. They had all been taken to the other side the night before, where the horsedealer had seen them, chained and pad-locked. Now, on the right bank they descried a number of armed men untying the boats and getting ready to cross the river. They were the King's men, and it was obvious that they were not in need of help. Further, when they saw the Protestants on the far bank, they took aim and fired a heavy volley. Now everything was clear. The King had turned traitor and there was but one thing to do: escape at top speed. They all ran back to their houses. Montgomery,[2] with his long military experience, at once gave the Pré-aux-Clercs as their rendezvous: it would have been far too dangerous to flee one by one.

What had happened meanwhile to Guise and his men? The young Duke, his uncle Aumale and the Chevalier d'Angoulême had decided to make for the Faubourg St Germain as soon as they had been warned that Maugiron and Claude Marcel's 1,000 men were late. Tavannes had sent across the river the 200 soldiers who had fired at the Protestants while they were getting into their boats, but the Faubourg St Germain had not been surrounded in time and it was now obvious that the only means of capturing the Huguenots over the river was by sending cavalry and not foot soldiers. That is why Guise and his companions had galloped through the narrow winding streets. To begin with, they wasted much time reaching the Pont-au-Change and then passing along the Rue St Barthélemy[3] to the Pont St Michel. On the way, they had collected the keys of the Buci gate. The Buci gate was already famous in the history of

[1] It stood more or less where the Institụt de France stands now.
[2] He was of Scottish origin. In 1559, he had accidentally killed Henri II when jousting with him.
[3] Today, the Boulevard du Palais.

93

Paris, for it was this way that in 1418, by the treachery of Perrine-Leclerc, that the Burgundians, under Villiers de l'Isle Adam, had entered the city and for three days had plundered and murdered. When Guise and his men reached it, clattering over the flagstones of the Rue St André-des-Arts, the key which they handed to the man in command of the group of soldiers did not open the lock; they had been given the wrong one! Someone was sent back to the City Hall at once to get the right key: 'it provided lazy men with plenty of time to get to horse'!

So much time that, at the Pré-aux-Clercs, Montgomery's appointed rendezvous, there were about 100 men: Caumont was there with a half-dozen followers. The one who had not come was La Force, though he had given warning to others. When Caumont, going back to the Pré-aux-Clercs, passed the Rue de Seine to collect his brother and his nephews, he had found La Force and his younger son Jacques-Nompar ready to mount; but the elder boy, Armand, was ill and unable to follow them. Father and brother eventually refused to leave him.

Caumont, broken-hearted, returned to the Pré-aux-Clercs and noticed that the streets were filling with arquebusiers with white crosses on their helmets. Then a little group of men rode in: Guise and his party, who had opened the gate at last. Montgomery, whose horse was a fiery, tireless Spanish jennet, stood up on his stirrups and made a gesture, motioning his men away. The 100 men clattered off at full speed.

About ten of them were cut down by Guise's men: those whose horses could not keep the pace. But Montgomery succeeded in getting the rest across Vaugirard and to the road to Chartres, towards the west and liberty. After several hours of hopeless pursuit, Guise arrived at Montfort l'Amaury and had to realize he was defeated. The only thing he could do was to summon a few Catholic gentlemen from the neighbourhood[1] and order them 'to act so that those running away could not escape', confessing at the same time that he was unable to catch them. Then, knowing well that his orders could not be carried out, he rode back to Paris. By that time the sun had risen and Claude Marcel and his militia, together with a rabble of burghers, beggars, soldiers, scoundrels, hideous hags and even children, had managed to catch up with the two wasted hours —wasted through the Queen-Mother's over-great haste.

[1] At St Cegier, for instance.

CHAPTER FOUR

'Kill! Kill!'

I T was not only the militia and the regular troops under the orders of Le Charron, nor even the other para-military armed groups under Marcel, who had been summoned by the bells. The whole city mob had gathered in the streets with the first light of dawn: fanatical monks and that anonymous blind, irresponsible and cruel rabble, more drunk with its own shouting and the sight of blood than with wine or spirits. White handkerchiefs, white scarves and white paper crosses had appeared everywhere. Orders had been shouted and repeated by hundreds and thousands of mouths, and gave some sort of organization to this bloody improvisation.

It was still very early. Coligny's body, beheaded by Petruzzi, was still lying in the courtyard of his house in the Rue de Béthisy. Guise and his men had already ridden towards St Germain-des-Prés, and on the way had summoned all the passers-by to assist them in their gory business. In the houses near the Admiral's groups of noblemen and soldiers were carrying on their sinister task: each had been provided with a list and was killing according to orders. But suddenly the district which had so far been combed only by 'organized' murderers was now invaded by a new gang. Now the massacre could not be limited—if it ever had been—to the killing of the 'leaders' and the wholesale butchery ordered by the King, under some vague medieval fiction of legality, could no longer be disguised.

The pack of hounds thirsting for blood had been loosed and could not be restrained, even if anybody attempted to do so. Charles IX knew well what happens under such circumstances when hunting. He was already compiling his *Livre du Roi Charles*, in which he was to describe the hunting and capture of stags.

First of all the mob wanted a good look at Coligny to make sure he was dead. Someone tore his gown open and everybody wanted to snatch a scrap of it. Coligny's body was displayed naked, showing his gaping wounds. Another man, with a sharp knife, obscenely mutilated the corpse, while others, possibly sorry not to have been the first to think of such a brilliant idea, tore off scraps of flesh. But most of them thought that there was no point in clawing at a dead body while there were so many living people on whom they could glut their morbid lust.

What was left of the Admiral stayed where it was for one more day. Later, other scoundrels were to tie a rope to the bloody remains, drag them across the city to the gallows at Montfaucon and, fixing the fragments grotesquely on butchers hooks, haul them to the top. This disgusting quartering had given the mob a taste of blood and now they went to lend a hand to the killers who were cleaning up in the Rue de Béthisy and the whole district beside the Louvre. La Rochefoucauld had just been stabbed at his home in the Rue de Prouvaires.[1] The howling mob pursued his servants to the top floor and hurled them down. They did the same at Téligny's house, but they slaughtered not only the noblemen; the Huguenot carpenter Le Normand suffered the same fate. Less than two hours after the alarm had been rung by the Marie at St Germain-l'Auxerrois, more than thirty corpses were already scattered on the pavement with broken skulls and shattered limbs—poor people, rich merchants, noblemen, all slain by a mob whose bloodthirsty rage and hatred were just beginning to be roused. Similar scenes were repeated elsewhere.

Three young witnesses

A few witnesses—all of them young—have left horrifying accounts of the early hours of this Sunday morning. Jacques-Auguste de Thou, a nineteen-year-old student, the son of the first President, related how, going to early mass, he saw people dragging the corpses of Jérôme Groslot, Baillif of Orleans, and of Calixe Carrault to the Seine to throw them in. He was obliged to watch this hideous spectacle without a tear, though

---

[1] In his *Evocation du Vieux Paris*, J. Hillaret mentions the fact that, in Louis XIV's reign, some 4,000 gold coins, dating from the reign of Charles IX, were discovered in a cellar in the Rue des Prouvaires: most likely they had been buried there at the time of the St Bartholomew massacre.

7 HENRI III in Venice (1574). Frescoe by Tiepolo. (Henri III is in mourning as his brother Charles IX has just died)

(Jacquemard-André Museum —Paris)

GASPARD DE SAULX, Seigneur de Tavannes. After a portrait by Tassaert

(Collection of M. G. de Villeneuve)

8 & 9 Eye-witness portrayal of the Massacre of Saint Bartholomew's Day, by François Dubois, a Huguenot refugee, who died in Geneva in 1584. *Lausanne Museum*

his tender nature did not allow him to watch the death of an innocent animal without being moved.[1]

Maximilien de Béthune, Baron de Rosny—later created Duke de Sully—was even younger in 1572: he was scarcely thirteen. He was awakened by the clanging bells at three in the morning and saw his tutor St Julien and his valet getting up to see what was the matter. Neither came back and Sully never knew what happened to them. His lodger, who was also a Protestant, begged him to go to mass to save his life. The boy thought it would be better to try and find shelter at the Collège de Bour-gogne.[2] He put on his scholar's gown, took a large missal under his arm as a sort of safe-conduct, and went out. In the Rue St Jacques, the Rue de la Harpe, and in the Cloister St Benoît, he came across groups of guards: each time his missal saved his life. On his way he saw the mob breaking into houses, looting them, murdering men, women and children, and yelling: 'Death to the Huguenots!'

When the boy reached his college, he had to argue for a long time with the porter and tip him heavily, and it was only after having been refused admittance twice that he was finally allowed to go to Principal La Faye's room. Carefully avoiding attracting the attention of two priests who were sitting with him and talking of putting all the Huguenots, including babes in arms, to the sword, La Faye managed to smuggle the boy into a secret closet, where he kept him hidden and fed for three days.

Another boy had an even more miraculous escape, and he also bore witness. He was Jacques-Nompar, the younger son of M. de la Force, who had remained in the Faubourg St Germain while the other Protestants were escaping under Montgomery's lead. Rather than leave his sick elder child, Armand, alone, La Force had refused to follow his brother and had gone back to his room with his two boys, praying and waiting for whatever God might please to send him. Just a few minutes after the Protestant squadron had ridden away, soldiers broke into the Rue de Seine lodgings, led by a Captain Martin who, brandish-ing his naked sword, ran into the room where La Force was sitting with his boys. In an effort to save them, the father uttered the word 'ransom', which gave the soldiers and their captain the idea of looting the place first: they took everything they could

[1] J. A. de Thou, *Histoire de ma vie*.
[2] It stood where the buildings of the Old Faculty of Medicine stand today.

lay their hands on, money, jewels and silver plate, and when they had collected all there was, they were again preparing to kill when La Force, for the second time, spoke of ransom, for he saw how very strong was their lust for gold. He mentioned an unbelievably high figure, 2,000 écus, something like twenty million francs. It was enough to induce the men to sheath their swords. In haste, they tore handkerchiefs to pieces to make arm bands for La Force, his boys, their page, La Vigerie, and their valet, Gast. They tied crosses to their hats and took them to Martin's house. They went down to the river, were rowed across and made their way to the Rue des Petits-Champs, where the captain lived. There they were left, guarded by two Swiss. La Force had asked for two days to collect the money.

During the short crossing of the Seine, the five Huguenots witnessed a fearful sight. The Seine was in the very centre of the slaughter area. Corpses were dragged to its banks, wounded people were dispatched there, and blood-splashed ferrymen took the bodies to the middle of the stream to tip them into the water. From the bridges, and preferably from the Pont-aux-Meuniers, murderers were throwing corpses into the water as the easiest way to get rid of them.

The Pont-aux-Meuniers

The last downstream bridge was the Pont-aux-Meuniers, linking the Conciergerie to the Châtelet. This was the place where dead or wounded victims were carried to be tipped into the river. Women were not spared: the Lady d'Yverny, who tried to escape in disguise with her daughters, was recognized by her fashionable coloured petticoat, which showed beneath her coarse woollen skirt. She was at once identified as a Protestant and surrounded by a yelling crowd. A man grabbed her and put the point of his dagger to her breast, shouting:

'Pray to the Holy Virgin and the saints, and you will be saved. If not . . .'

She scorned to demean herself by yielding to superstition and was stabbed at once, then dragged to the bridge and cast into the water. The Seine also bore along the corpse of her son-in-law Antoine de Clermont-Gallerande, Marquis de Resnel,[1] who,

---

[1] An extremely dashing, brave follower and friend of Condé. He fought at Dreux, Jarnac, Montcontour, Arnay-le-Duc. His wife was Anne de Longu-yon, and they had a son.

escaping to his house, clad only in his shirt, had been taken to the bank, thrown into a barge and stabbed by his own cousin, Bussy d'Amboise, who had recognized him.

On the bridge the murderers were making their victims walk the plank, as pirates did with the crews of captured ships. The wretched people were hoisted on to a window sill or on to the parapet and pushed into the stream. But because good swimmers might foster the faint hope of reaching the opposite bank they were stabbed before being thrown from the bridge, and when they reached the water and the splash had subsided, large red stains followed them downstream.

New groups kept arriving, dragging or pushing their victims along. In the Rue aux Ours, one such procession had formed round a button maker, Bertrand the Elder, and his apprentices, who were compelled at the point of the sword to walk to their death. They were all bled to death before being pushed into the river. Bertrand's wife had been spared that horrible walk: she had been killed on her doorstep and her murderers had not bothered to carry her body to the river. Two women were pushed in alive, the wife of the King's dealer in feathers and her maid (servants almost always shared their masters' fate). No one thought they could swim. By a miracle they rose to the surface; they were carried down by the current and washed towards some piles to which they clung. Then some lusty fellows dispatched them by stoning them from the bridges and the bank amidst roars of laughter, vying with each other as to who could throw best and who would be the first to force them to release their hold. . . .

The Pont Notre-Dame

Throughout the day the same hideous scenes took place on that bridge and the next, the Pont Notre-Dame, slightly further upstream in front of the Cathedral. Several Huguenot merchants and artisans lived in the houses and shops that stood on either side. Their doors were broken in at once and they were thrown down from their own windows. This is what happened to the ironmonger Mathieu, his wife and their lodgers, and also to the haberdasher Barthélemy du Tillet. Next door, at the Golden Cloak, all were put to the sword, men, women, children and servants. Another merchant who lived on the bridge, Nicolas le Mercier, was also stabbed and drowned, but not before he had seen his wife, his son-in-law, his daughter, his other children and his maid slaughtered before his eyes and thrown into the water.

Houses which had been emptied of their inhabitants were looted at once of anything valuable and even of heavy furniture. Not all the Parisians who went to the bridges were there to help in the slaughter and defenestration: some were there just to enjoy the sight, others came for a rest before going back to the kill. Some would recognize a victim and hurl abuse or a jest at him or her, and as if they were connoisseurs they would relish a few original ideas: a man had come from a house where, having butchered the tenant and his wife, had put their two little children into a basket and was much admired when he tipped them over the bridge from his back.

The 'August bleeding . . .'

The sun had now risen and the courtiers and members of the King's council were riding across Paris, admiring the frenzy of the mob that was ridding the kingdom of the heretic devils. Montpensier was cheered when he came along, shouting to all and sundry that to show their loyalty to the King they must strive to exterminate the Huguenots.

Tavannes—who later wrote in his memoirs that he had been one of the moderate members of the council!—had found a slogan he was so proud of that he went all over the city, shouting it at the top of his voice: 'Make them bleed! Bleeding is as wholesome in August as in May!'

Nevers was riding with a number of his retainers, and four or five of the accompanying noblemen had tall bewildered-looking men riding pillion behind them: they were English noblemen whose lives had been tactfully spared by the Duke. He had driven away the mob that was besieging their house, which they intended to defend to the death. But he thought it amusing to keep them captive for the whole day and compel them to witness the slaughter of their co-religionists. To begin with, he took them to the Rue de Bethisy early in the morning, to show them Coligny's mangled body.

'Do you recognize him?' Nevers asked one of the Englishmen.

'I have never seen him,' answered the man warily, thinking it safer than to confess that, on the contrary, he had known him well, having commanded a party of English volunteers under Coligny during the last war.

As for Anjou, he left the Louvre as soon as it was full daylight with a small army of 800 horsemen, 1,000 foot and four little field guns, in case of need, to raze any house in which Huguenots might entrench themselves. But he had nothing to do: the people who had been described as conspirators, ready to put Paris to fire and the sword, and whose criminal plans had to be forestalled, were not even on their guard. Very few of them sold their lives dearly.

Resistance

Yet, while so many of them were slaughtered like lambs, it is possible to cite instances of victims who fought to the end. Guerchy, for one, fought sword in hand before falling to sheer numbers.

The Strasbourg burgher[1] who was in Paris on August 23rd and 24th, witnessed a fight, the heroes of which he was unfortunately unable to identify. Three Huguenot gentlemen and a lady, who were staying at the Hôtel des Trois Rois, took refuge in the Jewellers' Chapel and there, well provided with ammunition, fired on their besiegers as long as their powder and bullets lasted. At the end, of course, they were literally torn to pieces.

Taverny, the lieutenant of police, assisted by one soldier, fought all day in his house, firing through the windows, and then, when his ammunition was exhausted, poured boiling pitch over his besiegers. They had to send for guards with steel armour and bucklers to break into the house. Finally, before being overwhelmed, Taverny fought on his doorstep, firing his two last pistol-shots first, then using his sword. When the King's soldiers broke into the house over his dead body, they had their revenge by pulling his grievously ill daughter out of bed and dragging her naked through the streets until she died. Taverny's wife, whom they found praying, sustained several wounds before being thrown into prison.

'Le chasseur déloyal'

Taverny's hopeless fight lasted well into the afternoon. Meanwhile, as the mob continued its murderous task and noblemen were parading through the city, let us see what the King was

[1] See note on p. 77.

doing at the Louvre, since it was by his authority that murder, torture and theft were made lawful.

Charles knew full well what he had done: he was taking all the credit for the scenes of horror which had occurred during the night and those which were taking place by day. Naked, mangled bodies were heaped beneath the windows, and the screams or dying groans of men, women and children were still ringing through the Palace as they were murdered before the King's eyes ... *Qualis artifex.* ... He had completely forgotten what he had felt the day before: his reluctance when the scheme was put to him and the fact that his mother had had some difficulty in getting him to agree to the slaughter. Now his lowest instincts, which he no longer attempted to hide, made him feel the same replusive glee as when ripping open a deer or a stag, except that now it was increased tenfold.

It was Charles who ordered that the corpses of the Huguenot noblemen he had known personally should be brought to the Louvre. Checking a list, he would get angry when captains were late and accounts of executions were slow to arrive. It was the King who ordered the storming of Taverny's house, and when he heard that there was some reluctance to murder Lavardin[1] he sent his own men to dispatch him. From time to time some marginal case was put to him or he was asked what to do with Huguenots caught alive, whether to kill them or send them to prison. He never hesitated: nothing but death would satisfy him. When he feared that the prisoners' keepers might show some pity, he sent his own men to watch the execution or, if necessary, carry it out.

This brings us to a question which has already provoked a long and heated controversy: did this murderous madman actually take his gun and, as Agrippa d'Aubigné wrote in his well-known account, 'shoot at those that passed who were too slow to drown'?[2] It may well be said that it is immaterial whether a King, who has already been guilty of the murder of so many of his subjects, did actually fire a few shots at them. It can also be said, as a learned German historian has done, that 'the arquebuse episode is both insufficiently proved or insufficiently denied'.[3] If one can rid one's mind of prejudices

[1] François de Beaumanoir, Sieur de Lavardin, 1532-1572, Henri de Navarre's tutor.
[2] In *Les Tragiques.*
[3] Soldan, *Frankreich und die Batholomaensnacht.*

which are rather aimless when so many years have elapsed, one must admit that the so-called 'legend' rests on very strong probability. Even if one does not wholly accept the arguments of Calvinist scholars, one must agree that one of them at least has gathered together a number of very conclusive arguments: this is Henri Bordier, who published *La Saint Barthélemy et la critique moderne* in 1874. It is true that a few contemporaries of the massacre do not mention the King's shooting. In a Protestant pamphlet, *Le tocsin contre les massacreurs*, even the following phrase concerning the King's behaviour is to be found: 'Not that he put his hand to it.' It is rather amusing to see that many Catholic writers have used that very quotation to whitewash Charles, after having denied any serious value to the *Tocsin* as an historical source. But, contrary to what has been too often repeated, the accusations were not found only in the *Réveille-Matin*, whence they were supposed to have been borrowed by other writers.

Of course, it is possible that Simon Goulart, Agrippa d'Aubigné, Brantôme (who was a Catholic) and later Mézeray, and even Bossuet, who also mentions that episode, not contesting its truth, may have borrowed it from one and the same source, the *Réveille-Matin*. However, it is a very valuable source, whether its author was, according to Bordier, the Dauphiny doctor Nicolas Barnaud,[1] who was with Coligny when he was wounded on the 22nd, or, as Joseph Barrère suggested a little later, François Hotman,[2] the author of *Francogallia*.

Yet one has no right to ignore another source, quoted in 1728 by Voltaire who, going further than Brantôme, wrote: 'Several persons have met a gentleman who was over a hundred years old and who had been in Charles IX's guard in his youth. He was asked questions about the St Bartholomew night, and whether it was true that the King had shot at fleeing Huguenots: "Sir, I did load his gun", answered the old man.' One may wonder with Bordier if it was not precisely because of the part played in the debate by Voltaire, that, in reaction against him

---

[1] A doctor born at Le Cret in Dauphiny at an unknown date. Very little is known about his life, but he published numerous books of religious controversy. He travelled widely, lived in Switzerland after the St Bartholomew massacre, and also went to England and Holland.

[2] 1524-1590. His family was of German origin. He studied law in Orleans and became a Protestant in or about 1546; he was with Calvin in Frankfurt, went back to France and attended Condé. He escaped to Switzerland in 1572, and lived in Geneva and afterwards in Basle.

and what he stood for, people began to argue a point which until then had been taken for granted, and which had been confirmed by Voltaire.

In his notes for *La Henriade*, Voltaire was a reliable historian. He never hesitated, when he thought he had made a mistake, to confess it, whether it concerned the words Charles IX is supposed to have uttered when he saw Coligny's corpse hanging at Montfaucon, or the story of Jacques-Nompar de La Force's escape. During the Revolution, the story of the King's shots was used for propaganda, and in the reaction the authenticity of the story was again questioned. The Convention had a plaque, with a fiery text, fixed above a window from which, under no circumstances whatever, could Charles IX have shot at anything, because it was not there in 1572. It provided a few conformist writers with a new argument: the King could not possibly have fired the shots as he had no window from which to fire!

It seems sensible to accept as a proven episode that glimpse of Charles IX firing at fleeing men and women, or at dead bodies drifting down the Seine. One must bear in mind that the King had a passion for forging weapons. It has to be taken along with several similar episodes, neither more nor less proved, but coming from similar original sources. One may quote, as it comes very handy, the anagram coined by the author of the *Réveille-Matin* who, according to the fashion of the time, was denouncing Charles IX through the very letters of his name: CHARLES DE VALOIS = LE CHASSEUR DÉLOYAL.

At the Palace

Charles IX had his mother near him all the time. She apparently did not yet suspect any political drawbacks to the operation she had designed and started. She was soon to realize that she might lose control over forces so carelessly unleashed. Yet for the present she was simply relishing, in her Italian ruthlessness, a sight which, to the eyes of history, was to be much worse than the Sicilian Vespers.

To please their mistress, and also because their perverted sensuality craved it, the beautiful maids of honour of the Queen's 'Flying Squadron' were watching the slaughter with smiles on their lips. They even went to take a close look at the naked corpses of Huguenot noblemen who had been flirting

with them the day before. It seems that, at Catherine's suggestion, some of those lovely girls had one of the bodies dragged
from under the heap in order to look at it more closely. This
was the corpse of Quellenec, Baron de Pont,[1] the husband of
Catherine de Parthenay-Soubise, and they wanted to look at it
because this was a man whose marriage had been annulled for
non-consummation.

The King, the Queen Mother, and their lords and ladies in
attendance, were out to enjoy the day and they did not want to
miss anything of the show. They ran from window to window,
calling to one another and crowding together whenever there
was anything out of the ordinary to see, either a cartload of
bodies being tipped into the river, or someone being forced to
death along the banks of the Seine. They were all laughing and
congratulating one another.

'Now the war is really over and we shall live in future in
peace.'

'This is how to make a real edict of pacification, not with
deputies and papers!'

They were vying with one another in cruelty, lubricity and—
let us hope—thoughtlessness: very few dared to differ from the
Queen Mother and the King and evince any human feeling when
faced with the blood-bath. Yet one woman refused to share in
the general glee, though she probably was the most devout
Catholic at court: Queen Elizabeth of Austria, the Emperor
Maximilian's daughter. 'When she woke,' wrote Brantôme, 'she
was told of the fine play that was being performed. "Alas", she
cried out, "does the King my husband know of it?" "Yes,
Madam", she was told, "and he has ordered it." "Oh my God!"
she exclaimed, "what does it mean? And which councillors gave
him such an advice? Oh my God! I implore and beg You to
forgive him! If You have no pity, I greatly fear his offence will
never be forgiven". And asking for her Book of Hours, she
began to meditate and pray to God, bitterly weeping.'

The King's youngest brother, Alençon, surprised everybody
by showing severe disapproval: Catherine knew what he thought
and had carefully avoided taking him to the various meetings
on the 23rd. In fact, as early as the morning of the 24th, he was

[1] Charles de Quellenec; he had been Condé's follower and friend through
several campaigns. He had married Catherine de Parthenay in 1568 when she
was thirteen, and he was killed before the legal decisions of the court in the
matter of non-consummation.

heard to say heedlessly that he could not approve of such disorder and of such a dastardly breach of faith. Such words gave much offence and Catherine, beside herself with rage, threatened to have him put into a sack and thrown into the Seine if he did not keep silent.

As for Marguerite de Valois, she was in a very uncomfortable position. She was a Catholic, still in love with Guise, but married against her will to a Huguenot; she did not disapprove of Coligny's murder, and she had said so quite openly. But she was also somewhat compassionate, and she derived no pleasure from this widespread butchery. She used her influence to save a few lives.

Navarre and Condé were still confined in the King's room, constantly taunted and abused by him, with no idea at all what their ultimate fate would be, and constantly told that men and women who were dear to them were on the list of victims. Besides their companions and friends who had come from distant provinces to attend their weddings, they mourned the death of some of their most faithful servants: Francourt, the late Queen of Navarre's chancellor, Le More, a pastor whom the young King completely trusted, and Caboche, his private secretary, had already fallen to the killers. Condé, moreover, had heard of the horrible death of Parenteau, his father's secretary, butchered in the Rue de la Vielle Monnaie, together with his wife, who was about to have a child.[1]

Looting begins

As the hours passed and the morning wore into the afternoon, the aspect of the massacre gradually changed. Of course, there were still shouts of 'Death to the Huguenot!' and there was not a thrust from dagger or sword that was not supposed to be punishment for heresy. But the reality was quite different. According to Tavannes, 'Paris was like a conquered city: once the blood was staunched, looting began'.

To say that blood was staunched is grossly optimistic: blood was going to flow for days after St Bartholomew. But it is quite true that looting had begun, and that the Paris mob and the soldiers were behaving exactly like a wild invading army before whom the gates of a long-coveted city had just been opened.

[1] The street disappeared in 1855 when the Boulevard du Centre—now the Boulevard de Sebastopol—was opened.

First they killed and then they looted; now they were killing in order to loot.

The sudden thirst for loot was noticed by all the witnesses: even by Tavannes, who hated the Huguenots, and by the Italians who were notorious papists. The Nuncio Salviati wrote at the end of the day: 'The Parisians have started looting with extraordinary greed. People who had never dreamt that they could own horses or silver plate have plenty of them tonight.'

The list of victims is revealing of what the murderers were after. A large number of jewellers, money-changers, and lapidaries were killed. Phillippe le Doux, the Queen-Mother's lapidary and all his family; Nicolas Dupuy's wife, who was looking after the jeweller's shop; Bourselle, another jeweller; Luffaut, jeweller and lapidary, together with his wife, children and lodgers; Jean de Cambrai, changer at the Palace of Justice; 'Little James', maker of gold thread—these are but a few of the murdered tradesmen. Of course, the gold and silver and precious stones found in their shops helped to strengthen the murderers' faith and zeal.

On the lowest level of society beggars, thieves, housebreakers and idlers of all descriptions were found busily robbing the dead. But such a splendid opportunity was not to be grasped only by the lowest of the low, by the usual gallows-birds who were suddenly given an opportunity to play the hangman's part. The King's soldiers were not the slowest to help themselves. A witness, who could not be suspected of Huguenot sympathies, as he was the Duke of Mantua's envoy, wrote: 'With my own eyes I saw the King's guards leading away horses and carrying bundles of silver plate and things of great value.' The King himself had recognized the Swiss guards' right to loot: as their special reward he gave them the house of the rich lapidary Thierry Badoire and all that was in it, valued at more than 2,000 écus.

Captain Martin, to pocket a ransom, agreed to spare La Force and his sons for the time being. A certain Captain Michel called early in the morning at the home of Pierre de la Place,[1] the President of the Court of Aids, and agreed to save his life for

---

[1] Pierre de la Place, 1520-1572. A very learned lawyer who had studied in Poitiers and published several legal books. He was superintendent of Condé's household. He was murdered and his library looted. His daughter and his son-in-law succeeded in purchasing their lives.

1,000 écus. Later in the day, other soldiers called again, and this time they were led by the Provost Séneçay and Lieutenant Toutevoye. Pretending to protect La Place, they settled into his house, and La Place saw at once that it would cost him much more than 1,000 écus to get rid of them.

The greatest and the richest noblemen did not evince less greed and they no more sought to hide their sordid rapaciousness than did the rabble and the soldiery. For instance, Retz indulged in a revolting piece of blackmail on Loménie, who was compelled to give him his estate in Versailles and to sell him his post as secretary to the King, and was none the less done to death as soon as the deeds had been completed. It was the same with poor people: Maupelé and his wife were hastily dispatched by Guise's assassins because they had been impudent enough to start a lawsuit against him. As for Bussy d'Amboise, in killing his cousin the Marquess de Resnel, he made use of convenient circumstances to give a profitable end to a lawsuit between himself and his victim over a fat inheritance.

The King himself set the example: from early morning he had his secretaries draw up a list of the offices that were falling vacant, because of the deaths of their holders, and he was already concerned with getting good money for them. One understands why Mézeray wrote: 'If one had money, or a well-paid office, or dangerous enemies, or hungry heirs, then one was a Huguenot.' The names can be given of some devout Catholics who, in spite of their religion, were also thrown into the Seine: Rouillard, for instance, a church councillor who was suing a colleague for forgery; Villemor, son of a former Keeper of the Seals and *Maître des requêtes*, who was also suing a shady colleague; even a Spaniard, the Lord of Salcede, a sworn enemy of the Huguenots but a man who was on bad terms with the Cardinal of Lorraine—his properties were looted and duly carried to the Guise mansion by his murderers.

Divided families

Mézeray might have made a note of the fact that hatred as well as greed armed the killers and informers. Family hatred is often the worst, the most lasting and the most cruel. Here are a few instances from a wide choice: the hatred of a husband for his wife, a wife for her husband, a daughter for her mother.

The case of Commissioner Aubert may be cited, who lived

near the Fontaine Maubuée.[1] His wife was Protestant, and he was Catholic, but that is not enough to explain—let alone to exculpate—the husband's attitude. He first tried to have her converted by a Sorbonne monk,[2] who obviously was not interested in leading her to a genuine conversion, and merely told her that she would save her life by attending mass.

'My life,' she answered, 'is not dear enough to me that I should become an idolator in order to save it.'

St Bartholomew's day provided Aubert with a good opportunity to test her faith and get rid of this Huguenot wife. He drove her out of the house at the height of the massacre and delivered her to the mob who 'stoned and cudgelled her to death, committing all sorts of inhumanities on her body'. After which Aubert thanked the murderers who had killed his wife.

On the other hand, it was through his wife that a poor and aged carpenter of the Rue d'Espronnelles met his death. They were not living together and, while he continued to live at his shop, she had gone to live at the home of a relative near the Coûture Ste Catherine.[3] Early in the morning, the man had been dragged out of bed by the murderers who, doubtless through thoughtlessness rather than pity, had thrown him alive into the river from the Pont-aux-Meuniers. He managed to swim across, climbed up the big piles of the bridges and, stark naked and shivering, reached the Marais without being caught again, so as to beg his wife for shelter. But without even opening the door or handing him a garment, she drove him away. The poor man, 'not knowing where to go, dragged himself along in that condition, and at daybreak was caught again and drowned'.[4] As for Jean de Coulogne's wife she might have escaped as those who were looking for her could not find her hiding place, but she was given away by her daughter, who later married one of her murderers.

Anxiety at the City Hall

So far the court had felt no anxiety at seeing a gigantic auto-da-fé turned quickly into wholesale looting and robbery, mixed with a few sordid private murders. Yet it soon brought dismay

[1] One of the three oldest fountains in Paris, which stood where No. 121 Rue St Martin now is.
[2] Mentioned in *Le tocsin contre les massacreurs*.
[3] Now Rue Sévigné.
[4] Quoted by *Le tocsin*.

to the hearts of rich merchants and burghers who were the administrative body at the City Hall.

It seems that their militia and companies, though they had taken part in the early morning executions, had not had much to do with subsequent looting. Merchants and artisans, sitting there as aldermen, realized with a shock that their own class—the rich upper middle class—hated by the badly paid shop assistants and workmen, were paying the price of the massacre. Shopkeepers, especially, had been slaughtered because their shops could afterwards be looted. At the City Hall, Provost Le Charron, who was receiving news from all quarters, quickly realized that white crosses would soon mark, not only Huguenot houses, but those of all rich people. It was high time to act. At eleven o'clock the Provost and his aldermen arrived at the Louvre.

The City Clerk has written in his register the result of the interview: 'On the said day of St Bartholomew, between eleven and twelve in the morning, the King listened to the observations made by the said Provost and Aldermen, purporting to the fact that princes, princesses and lords of his court, gentlemen, archers, soldiers of his guard and attendants and all sorts of people, and rabble under their protection, did loot and plunder houses and kill people in the street. . . . His Majesty was pleased to order the said Provost and aldermen to take to horse and get themselves accompanied by all the forces of the said city, and have all murders, looting, plundering and rebellion stopped at once, and see to it day and night.'

Accordingly, by midday, a general order to 'cease fire' had been given.

CHAPTER FIVE

The Pack is Cast off

To obey the King's order, Le Charron and his aldermen 'went round the city all day, escorted by the city militia, to restrain everybody and to stop and prevent murder, looting and pillage'. If one confined oneself to the 'registers and chronicles of the city offices', one might believe that their rounds, carried out to the sounding of trumpets and with all the usual ceremonies, re-established order in Paris at once. In fact the Provosts and aldermen are said there 'to have brought such good order about that everything should have died down and ceased at once'.

'At once' was, however, not the right phrase, for the next paragraph reveals how the city councillors were greeted by the Paris mob in spite of their trumpets and proclamations: 'Their rounds were carried out by the said Provost and aldermen in person with the city captains, archers, arquebusiers and arbalesters, all through the night and also the days and nights that followed, without ceasing, until everything had calmed down and they had seen peace restored in the city.' Such is the sad truth.

Paris had broken loose and had tasted blood and pillage: it was not to be stopped before it was worn out, disgusted and exhausted. That stage had not yet been reached at noon that Sunday.

What the City Council feared had happened: middle-class people, whether Huguenot or lukewarm Catholics, were now providing the greater number of victims. The killers, made insensitive by the extent of their crimes, spared no one when attacking a family. There were as many children as adults among the dead. In the Rue St Marceau, after having killed a cobbler and his wife, the murderers hacked their three children to pieces; a gilder, Guillaume Maillart, was slaughtered with his wife and their little son; in the Rue St Martin a hat maker had her two children killed before her eyes and was then stabbed to death; in the Rue St Denis, at the Hart's Horn, the three children of a silk merchant were butchered on their parents' bodies. Sometimes, those hideous scenes went on endlessly and reached the pitch of horror. While a horse dealer, repeatedly stabbed, was dragged to the Seine, his two children clung to him, weeping and screaming. The awful procession reached the Seine and, after having thrown the poor man into the river, the murderers got rid of the children by stabbing them and drowning them too. A moment later, a man covered with blood up to his bristling beard came out of a house, within which he had obviously slain all the occupants. He was carrying in his arms— to toss him into the Seine—a baby who was gaily laughing and playing with his executioner's beard. That did not move the brute's heart; when he reached the bridge, he plunged his dagger into the baby's belly and threw him into the river, uttering fearful blasphemies all the time.

Children were not victims only. Some of them, who were used to playing in the gutter, were proud to ape their elders and felt at home at once in the unusual atmosphere that reigned over their normal playground. Some did no worse than grab what had been overlooked in looted houses, but others went further and boys of nine and ten were seen in the street, dragging a baby in swaddling clothes like a wooden doll, round whose neck they had tied a belt.

'The paper would weep,' wrote Simon Goulart, 'were I to attempt to write all the shameful blasphemies uttered by those devils and monsters in the heat of the slaughter.' It would probably weep more bitterly still at the account of some of the episodes Simon Goulart himself recorded.

Children, as we have just seen, were not spared, neither were pregnant women. Here are a few instances. In the Rue de la Huchette, at the sign of the Star, a woman big with child was murdered; so was Antoine Saunier's wife, who was stabbed and drowned. In the Rue St Martin a woman who was about to give birth to her child escaped through the garret of her house and got on the roof, but she was found there and killed; her belly was ripped open and her child smashed against a wall. The Strasbourg burgher saw a countess stripped of her fine garments and jewels, stabbed and finally thrown into the river. She too was pregnant, and so near her term that one could see her child moving. And Parenteau, the late Prince of Condé's secretary, was killed with his wife, who was also about to give birth to her child.

The hatred for learning

The day was drawing to a close when killers and thieves, almost sated with their feats, suddenly remembered some of the curses lately uttered by fanatical preachers from the pulpit. The day would lose part of its meaning and Paris would not be completely cleansed, nor heresy wiped out, if for some unknown reason they continued to spare the University district, where French and foreign students were taught in defiance of the Sorbonne worthies.[1] Those students were likely to provide the next generation of heretic ministers.

By that time the scholars or those who were working for them had already been decimated. The wife of Jean Borel, a bookseller, had been stabbed instead of her husband, who had not been found, and his books had been burned; so were the Bibles which were bound by Richard Breton, and his apprentice was killed. As for Spire Niquet, a poor binder and father of seven children, he was roasted alive over a fire made of his books in front of his shop in the Rue Judas.

All that was nothing compared with what took place in the Latin quarter, towards which the mob was hurrying. To begin with, they looted and destroyed booksellers' shops, not caring in the least whether they sold forbidden books such as the Psalms in French and Huguenot Bibles, or merely pious books duly approved by the archbishop. In the Rue St Jacques, Oudin kept a small shop: he was well known as a devout Protestant. Together with a professor and a pastor of Spanish origin, he was dragged to the river of purification. The author of the *Déluge*, a doggerel poem, describes that feat in the following way:

> *Un Abrahan grand pédagogue,*
> *D'enseigner avait grosse vogue*
> *Ses disciples à la huguenotte;*
> *Mais il marcha en même flotte*

[1] The Sorbonne was the school of divinity, well-known for its narrow-mindedness. It was violently hostile to the Collège de France, far more liberal-minded.

Que le petit Odin, libraire,
Et après eux on voyait braire
Un de Lopes espagnol ministre
Guerdonné de sa vie sinistre.[1]

The Spaniard Lopez was not the only foreigner who went down during the fateful day. Besides his countryman Salcède—the Cardinal of Lorraine's private enemy—various Italians, not all of whom appeared to have embraced the Protestant faith, were killed and robbed: Maphé from Venice, Simon from Lucca, Lazare Romain from Piedmont. Three Englishmen also perished. Yet eighteen-year-old Philip Sidney, whose parents had sent him to the Continent to complete his education and gather some experience of foreign countries, was lucky enough to escape to the English Embassy, where Walsingham sheltered him.

The mob raced up the narrow streets of the Montagne Ste Geneviève, which they usually avoided, and the list of victims grew longer and longer, as informers were quick to give the label 'Huguenot' to German or Flemish students. Doubtless, a few 'errors' were committed which would help to give easier access for certain candidates to their coveted chairs.

A good instance of the hatred raging between scholars—almost the equal of the congugal hatred cited earlier—deserves to be mentioned: the rivalry between the great philosopher Pierre de la Ramée (called Ramus) and Charpentier, the leader of the University Aristotelians. Ramus had begun life as a servant in the College de Navarre, and it was only through his exceptional talent that he rose to the post of Royal Reader at the Collège de France, and then Principal of the Collège de Presle. Kings had called on him in his small garret in the Rue des Carmes; he was known and respected all over Europe.[2] His reputation came from the soundness of his dialectics, and the leading part he played when attacking the old scholastic and empirical doctrines. Michelet has written: 'Ramus deserved death on three different grounds: because he had shattered the

---

[1] 'A certain Abraham was a great scholar and he prided himself on teaching the New Learning to his students. But he was thrown into the same water as little Odin, the bookseller; after them they also tipped over, braying his head off, Lopez, a Spanish pastor who thus ended his disgusting life.' J. Copp de Vellay, *Déluge des Huguenots avec leur tombeau et les noms des chefs en principaux, punis à Paris le 24e jour d'Août et autes jours ensuivants.*

[2] He was Philip Sidney's professor and intimate friend.

power of Aristotle the Scholastic, because he had brought the harmonious unity of the sciences back to teaching, and because he had raised French to the rank of a scholarly language.' His rival, Charpentier, held over him a terrible weapon: Ramus was a Calvinist and he, Charpentier, was one of the Guise's henchmen. Thanks to Guise, he had been made a doctor when barely twenty-five. He was a rich man, so that he was able to buy in the Collège de France a chair in which he was supposed to comment on the works of Greek mathematicians, though he boasted that he knew neither Greek nor mathematics; he had finally left the University, where he was not missed, and joined the city militia of which he was made a captain.

After the Peace of St Germain, Ramus had returned to Paris and Charpentier had already succeeded in having his reinstallation at the Collège de France refused in defiance of the Edict. On August 24th, as soon as the mob had broken into the Latin quarter, Charpentier, while remaining carefully in the background, started a search for Ramus; this time he hoped to be rid of him for good. But when the killers arrived at the Collège de Presle, they found the garret empty. Yielding to his disciples' plea, Ramus had agreed to go into hiding in a cellar in the Rue St Jean de Beauvais. While the looters were ransacking a bookshop upstairs, Ramus had reason to believe that death had passed him by. The next day, he went back to his college.

Crime's 'Roll of Honour'

So far we have named a large number of victims, but the killers were mostly the anonymous mob or little groups of unidentified men. It is obvious that when a whole city is transformed into a many-headed beast of prey, and its worst instincts break loose, when tens of thousands of men, women and even children are out to run down, murder and despoil some hundreds of their fellow men, it is easier to make a list—though incomplete—of the victims than of the murderers.

Yet a few names stand out from this confused, anonymous mass: a few men whose cruelty was so exceptional that, even in the midst of savagery, it could not go unnoticed. Though it does not imply that there was any 'hierarchy' in crime, among the repellent heroes of that day of days one must mention a maker of gold thread named Crucé by some authors,[1] Thomas by

[1] De Thou.

others,[1] or simply the Maker of Gold Thread.[2] J. A. de Thou described him in the following way: 'I remember having seen this Crucé several times, and always with horror. The man, whose face was really that of a hangman, used to show his naked arm and relate that on St Bartholomew's day this arm had butchered more than 400 gentlemen.'

Crucé was probably exaggerating when he gave the title 'gentlemen' to all his victims, but if one checks the almost identical terms in which other contemporaries describe his nauseating attitude, it seems that the figure at least was correct. L'Estoile relates that this man killed the church councillor Rouillard, a canon of Notre-Dame and a devout Catholic. He cut the canon's throat after having kept him prisoner for three days, and he then dropped him into the Seine through a trapdoor in his own house, which was obviously built on one of the bridges.

This Crucé was an addict to crime since, much later, when this devil had turned hermit—in the proper sense—and gone to live in a desert region, he was, according to de Thou again, accused and almost convicted, together with several other hermits who lived in the same place, of murdering a Flemish merchant who had taken shelter in his cell.

There are only a few details concerning other killers, yet Jean Ferrier, a lawyer and a captain from the Rue St Antoine, was also outstanding for his cruelty. His Catholic zeal was far from being disinterested since, a few years later, on November 15, 1578, he was arrested and imprisoned in the castle of Loches for being a paid agent of Spain.[3] A butcher and another captain of the militia, named Perou, boasted of having slaughtered Huguenots like cattle. He reckoned that he killed and threw into the Seine 180 Protestants: a modest claim, compared with Crucé's 400!

Tanchou has also been listed as an 'elite' killer. He did his job in the prisons. For the prisons—the Châtelet and the Fort l'Evêque, especially—were full of Protestants, most of them having spontaneously sought refuge and protection there. Tanchou displayed his talents in making room for newcomers. Some days he killed as many as fifteen prisoners. Once, on

---

[1] Pierre de l'Estoile.
[2] Simon Goulart.
[3] Pierre de l'Estoile, *Journal de Henri III*.

Retz' behalf, he compelled Loménie to give up his estate and made him sign the deeds; then he strangled him.

René, the Queen-Mother's perfumer, must also be mentioned. L'Estoile describes him as: 'a man addicted to all sorts of shameful and cruel deeds, who used to visit prisons to stab Huguenot captives, and thrived on murder, theft and poisoning'. Public rumour accused him—possibly erroneously—of having poisoned Jeanne d'Albret a few days before the wedding of her son, the King of Navarre.

Simon Goulart gives other details of René's activities on August 24th: 'He lured a jeweller to his house pretending to save his life; he got him to give him all his merchandise, then cut his throat and threw him into the Seine.'

Finally, a nobleman deserves to be listed with the maker of gold thread, the butcher and the perfumer; the handsome Count Mark-Hannibal de Coconas. According to L'Estoile, who heard of it through Henri III, the Piedmontese prided himself on having ransomed out of his own pocket more than thirty Protestants, in order to extract a special pleasure out of them: he tortured them, then he offered them their lives if they recanted, and finally stabbed them whether they had perjured themselves or not. But not with one blow, as coarse people without taste or manners might do; he killed them slowly, with little stabs, to make them languish in agony, getting his own pleasure to the full at the same time.

M. de la Force's ransom

Mark-Hannibal de Coconas was to play his part within the next day or two in the house in the Rue des Petits-Champs where La Force and his sons had been taken by Captain Martin after he had agreed to the offer of ransom.

But for the moment, no one in the house in the Rue des Petits-Champs was thinking of this good-looking Piedmontese nobleman, a close friend of the King's brother and a great success with the court ladies. La Force, his sons, their page La Vigerie, and even the two Swiss guards who had become quite friendly with their captives, were thinking only of the mission entrusted to the valet Gast. He had been sent to the Arsenal by his master to contact Jeanne de Brisanbourg, the sister of Biron, Grand Master of the Artillery and the widow of a brother of both Caumont and La Force. La Force hoped she could collect the 2,000 écus he had promised Captain Martin. She actually gave her promise to the trusted servant: on Tuesday the 26th he would be able to take to his master the money to buy his own and his sons' lives. Yet Mme de Brisanbourg was very worried. She knew that at the Louvre it was rumoured that neither La Force nor his sons had joined Caumont and escaped with Montgomery's party. There was some talk about a mysterious hiding place. Now, in the King and Anjou's circle a captain of the guards, M. de Larchant, was moving heaven and earth to discover the truth, as he wanted to make sure that La Force, and above all his sons, should not escape the massacre.

The reason was that he had married the boys' half-sister, a daughter of Mme de la Force by her first husband, the unfortunate La Chataigneraye, who had been killed by M. de Jarnac in one of the most spectacular duels in history.[1] Consequently, M. de Larchant was most anxious to have the two little brothers killed. It will be remembered that Mézeray wrote that the mere fact that one had 'hungry heirs' was enough to have anybody dealt with as if he were a Huguenot; the more so if he really did belong to the reformed church. Consequently, in spite of the fact that they knew that the money was forthcoming, the inmates of Martin's house were far from feeling relieved. Yet La Force, who had sworn not to escape, refused to run away, in spite of the entreaties of his sons, his page, his valet and of the two Swiss. They had to wait until the 26th.

Back to politics

The afternoon was drawing to a close. The early excitement at the Louvre was over. The King was surrounded by his secret council: his mother, his brother Anjou, the Italians, Tavannes. Under the Palace windows, for the third time since midday, the city heralds, riding ahead of the aldermen and Provosts, had risen on their stirrups and sounded their trumpets. The orders of the King and of the Provost had been read in ringing voices. To everyone present the proclamation brought a kind of relief: it was not possible that such a solemn and stern declaration could be disobeyed. Even in the immediate entourage of the King and his mother there were those who thought it was high time. Tavannes said so: 'Once the deed was done, anger calmed and danger passed, sober minds realized that it had been more

[1] In 1547, in the presence of Henri II.

dangerous and formidable than was at first thought. The blood that had been spilled hurts one's concience.'

Such considerations might be termed 'moral' if one was not aware of the active part which Tavannes, with his 'sober' mind, had taken in the slaughter. Yet, apart from them, certain more political ideas were weighing on the councillors' minds and made them anxious that the summons to peace should be heard. They had seriously feared that they might be overwhelmed by an irresistible popular movement. Now, they felt relieved, as if they had passed very near to catastrophe, but had avoided it. The only thing now was to make the best possible use of the new situation.

Catherine was thoroughly pleased: within less than twenty-four hours she had regained control over the King's mind and will, and she was sure that it was for ever. She had to use her new-found power without delay. She was tenacious. Despite many reverses she had never lost sight of her original plan, which was to get rid both of the Chatillons and the Guises. It was not possible just now—at least, not today—to score twice. But now that the Protestant party was beheaded, why not start working at once to overthrow the other house? It only required some astuteness, plenty of bad faith, a little cunning, many lies and plenty of impudence, gifts with which Catherine knew she was well endowed. What would Machiavelli have said under such circumstances? Some of his well-cast sentences, summing up his ideas, rang in her mind: 'The only Princes who have done great things are those who have been able to deceive others. . . . One must be ready to feign and dissemble. . . . One who is out to deceive will always find someone who is willing to be deceived.'

She made a final declaration, when dismissing the council: 'Letters must leave today for the governors of the provinces and the ambassadors. The King shall write and so shall I, so that no one can doubt that we are in complete agreement over what has been done today, and what we think of it. . . . The thing to emphasize is the rivalry between the houses of Guise and Chatillon.'

Accordingly, the same evening, messengers left, carrying to far-away provinces and foreign capitals what was for the time being the official version of the event. One must read in full one of those letters in which, though signed by Charles IX, Catherine's voice can be heard from the first line to the last:

'My cousin,[1]

'You have heard what I wrote to you the day before yesterday, concerning the wound inflicted on my cousin the Lord Admiral, and how I was afterwards ready to do everything possible to clear things up and have the culprits punished, so that it should not be forgotten.

'Since then, it has so happened that those of the House of Guise, and other lords and gentlemen who are their adherents, and whose party is not inconsiderable in this city, as everyone knows, having known for sure that the said Admiral's friends wished to be revenged on them for his wound, were so angry last night that a great and lamentable rebellion broke out between them.

'Having broken through the guard which had been put round the Admiral's house to protect him, [they] killed him, together with several gentlemen, and others have also been killed in various parts of the city . . . which went on with such fury that, in order to keep myself and my brothers safe in my palace of the Louvre, the only remedy was to send out my guards and other forces and later to send out an order throughout the city to suppress the rebellion which, thank God, has now subsided, it having been caused by a long and private quarrel between the two houses.

'Having always foreseen that it would lead to more dangerous situations, I have done all I could to pacify the city, as everybody knows; there is no question of breaking the Edict of Pacification which, on the contrary, I want to enforce as much as ever.

'As it is greatly to be feared that such an execution will rouse my subjects against one another, and lead to great massacres in the cities of my kingdom, which I would regret very much, I request you to proclaim that every man must remain quiet and safe in his own house, refraining from taking arms or offending one another, on pain of death, thereby observing and keeping carefully the Edict of Pacification.'

Instructions followed, requesting Governors to collect as many troops as they could, and to send reports of the measures taken.

---

[1] This letter was sent to the Governor of Burgundy but all the letters sent to other Governors, those of Touraine and Poitou, for instance, are identical.

Is there anything to be said about this letter, apart from stressing its perfection? It is, without doubt, a masterpiece of political duplicity, of which there are few parallels in history. It lacks nothing: neither a reference to the King's attitude after Maurevert's crime, nor a hint at the Guises' dangerous power, nor the vain attempt made at protecting the Admiral (that is where Cosseins comes in), nor a picture of the poor King entrenched in his palace while the factions grapple with one another, nor the relief at the restoration of peace, thanks to the King . . . and to God. And above all, the resolve to maintain the Edict of Pacification.

The King had sent letters to the Ambassadors, telling more or less the same story in more or less the same words. Yet, when writing to those who might have to answer further questions put to them by Protestant sovereigns, he added that 'he had with him his beloved brother the King of Navarre and his dear cousin the Prince of Condé, who were sharing his fortune'; also 'how very much displeased he had been to see that, after so many attempts to bring about a sincere reconciliation between the Duke de Guise and the Admiral, it had all been to no purpose . . .'

The same messengers also bore letters to the same effect signed by Catherine, and proclamations endorsed by the Secretary of State Pinart, according to which it was forbidden to carry weapons or to gather in large groups, or do anything against the Edict.

Thus the Guises were made the scapegoats of the whole massacre. Their guilt would be even more obvious if, as was suggested to him, Duke Henri could be got quietly out of Paris. The King would then pride himself in having restored order. But two things were necessary if this cunning scheme were to succeed: Guise must be silly enough to bear the whole responsibility for the crime by keeping silent or going away, and Paris must be wise enough to go back to normal by the next morning.

Vixen v. fox

Guise had just ridden home: he was dead tired, exhausted and annoyed, following the fruitless ride that had occupied the whole day and had left him empty-handed.

Yet, when his men came to him and related the horrors which had taken place in Paris from dawn till dusk, Guise no longer regretted the escapade. Without seeking to ascribe to this young man more heart or more brains than necessary, we have to recognize that, despite an Italian mother, he was not cast in the same mould as the Valois.

He was vindictive and cruel, which had been amply revealed by his attitude in the Rue de Béthisy a few hours earlier. But he was a warrior. If he had been eager to murder Coligny, it was because, according to the so-called 'moral' code of the time, he thought that he was doubly justified: he was carrying out rightful vengeance upon the man whom he regarded as the instigator of his father's murder, and he was obeying the express orders of the King, who was supposed to have complete power over all his subjects. When he had rushed to St Germain-des-Prés and then along the road to Chartres in pursuit of Montgomery and his men, it was because he saw there the chance of a fair fight among gentlemen, a pleasant pastime on a fine August day.

But what had taken place meanwhile in Paris was neither a nobleman's, nor even a soldier's job.

Furthermore, Guise, who by all accounts was both well informed and well advised, heard that the Queen Mother was about to broadcast her own story of the massacre throughout the kingdom and abroad, showing it as the regrettable result of a long and private quarrel between the house of Lorraine and that of Chatillon and Montmorency. Messengers from Court had already told Guise's advisers that the Duke would do well, both for his own and the kingdom's good, to retire to his estates for some time. They added that the Marshal de Montmorency and his brothers had emerged unscathed from this bloody affair and it was feared that they might not be long in making the murderer of the Admiral, their uncle, and of many of their friends, feel the weight of their anger.

But the trick was too crude, and it did not take the Lorraine princes—Guise and his uncle d'Aumale—long to realise that the best way to bring Montmorency's hatred to bear upon them was to admit by flight their part in a crime for which they were only partly responsible. They immediately decided how to act and how to counter Catherine's Machiavellian plans.

The author of the *Rèveille-Matin*—who cannot be suspected of any weakness for the Guises—gave a striking summary of the newly created situation: 'The Guises,' he wrote, 'seeing the dreadful things that had happened, and realizing that they would draw on themselves and their descendants the anger of all humane men, as the only guilty persons, and foreseeing what a grievous position they would be in, went back to Paris and refused to leave the court, demanding, on the contrary, that the King should confess to all he had done.'

More than that: not content with violating the King's orders —or, at least with not deferring to his wishes—the Duke de Guise, though he was a devout Catholic, ready to fight the heretics on the battlefield, actually opened the gates of his home to devout Protestants, and saved their lives. Thus he gave refuge to Michel de l'Hôpital's daughter, and to the Seigneur d'Acier,[1] who later, it is said, gave his soul in exchange for his body. According to Mézeray, more than a hundred Protestants found refuge behind the heavy gates of the former Hôtel de Clisson.

Goulart, without quoting any figure, emphasizes the shrewdness of the Duke's mercifulness: 'It was with great cunning that the Guises saved several noblemen of the reformed faith, for by so doing they diverted all the fury on the King and his secret council, and acquired friends while ruining their enemies, and thereby showed that they were against the Admiral alone, because of their private quarrel.' Yet as a Protestant Goulart was not taken in. 'However,' he continued, 'they and their followers had been the first and most outstanding perpetrators of the massacre.'

Anyway, Charles IX, expressing doubtlessly his mother's disappointment, could not conceal his anger. 'The King took their courtesy very ill and reproached the Guises for it, saying that they had spared the lives of people who might take their own later on.' It is a pity that no one knows for sure whether Anjou—who was to become Henri III—was there when the King suggested that Guise might die a violent death.[2]

Through the meshes of the net

The Guises were not the only ones who, by the end of the day, were preparing the dossier to prove their double dealing, when tried by History, or—one never knows—some less distant judicial body. This was not surprising. Often, one or two cunningly selected human lives can weigh more on that strange scale than

[1] Jacques de Crussol, Seigneur d'Acier, second son of the Duke de Crussol. He had served under Condé and Coligny, and taken Andelot's post when the Admiral's brother had died. He was to abandon Protestantism in 1578. His brother Charles was killed during the massacre.

[2] He had Henri de Guise murdered in Blois on December 23, 1588.

an endless list of anonymous victims. A number of people endeavoured to save some convenient Huguenot before nightfall. It might be either a Huguenot or a tepid Catholic whom the King or the mob had entered in the list of the doomed. In that case, absolution would be easier still. Anjou, for a smile of his mistress, Renée de Rieux de Châteauneuf, saved the Marshal de Cossé, who otherwise 'would have gone down with the rest'. Claude Marcel, who had worked so hard to compensate for the laziness of Provost Le Charron, did something to ingratiate himself with one of the brothers Montmorency. Meeting Thore,[1] the youngest, during his morning round, he told him: 'If you care for life, go away at once. Paris is not going to be wholesome for members of your family today.'

As for Tavannes, whose memoirs were to help his descendants at Court—Henri IV's court, of course—he did not limit himself to one rescue. He produced a whole list. According to him, he saved La Neufville, Béthunes, Baignac and the Grand Master of the Artillery Biron, who was suspected of favouring the Huguenots. He saved him by advising him to take refuge in the Arsenal. Tavannes also prided himself on having striven to save Laverdin. As for the latter, the certain fact is that, in spite of such doubtful help, he was duly stabbed and thrown into the Seine from the Pont-aux-Meuniers. The only one who seems to have shown any compassion for this much respected old man was Captain Pierre Loup who, trying to play for time, answered those who were hurrying him and asking him what he was waiting for: 'I am waiting until I am really angry.' But the victim was torn from him and, in spite of Tavanne's supposed assistance, died that August 24th.

As for the future Marshal de Biron, he does not seem to have waited for Tavannes' advice to remove himself to the Arsenal. Early that morning, the Grand Master of the Artillery had taken the precaution of having four strong field guns trained upon the four possible approaches. That was enough to turn the Arsenal that day into one of the few almost inviolable refuges in Paris.

When comparing them with noblemen who, like Guise or Tavannes, calculatingly saved a few lives, one is tempted to find more honesty in a few blackguards who allowed Huguenots to buy back their lives and, once they had pocketed the ransom,

---

[1] Thoré became a Protestant shortly afterwards. He died in 1593.

had respected the bargain. One such was a captain of the Scots Guards who, in exchange for a heavy purse, allowed the Seigneur d'Argenlieu to slip away, after he had been brought to the Louvre and sentenced to death by the King in person. Yet the captain could easily have taken the purse from the man's dead body.

Side by side with these various rescues, carried out for more or less sordid ends, there were a few cases less rare, we hope, than the chronicles of the time would lead us to believe, where people, without calculation or ulterior motive, showed a little pity, even if they happened to be on the side of the killers.

Captain La Cornière, who was in command of the Swiss Guard in the Louvre, saw several wounded Huguenots who were pretending to be dead and had been thrown on to the pile of corpses, soon to be covered by others. He not only said nothing when he saw them emerge from under the mass of bodies, but he helped and protected those who were badly wounded, simply saying to his men: 'I believe that all these Huguenots will rise from the dead.'

Others spiced their work of mercy with a certain amount of theatrical display, either because they thought that these heretics did not all deserve death, but nevertheless could be given a good fright, or even more simply because, even in these macabre circumstances, they had a taste for jokes. One of these unpleasant suspense stories has been related by Mergey, who was the hero of it. After having heard Guise and his party riding away towards St Germain, he had sent his valet Vinat to look for La Rochefoucauld's young son. He had stimulated the man's zeal by presenting him with a fat purse and had assured his safe-conduct by tying a handkerchief round his arm and sticking a white paper cross to his hat.

Vinat found the young count—who had just come into the title through the charming 'Foucauld's' death—sheltering with his tutor, M. de la Coste, at the lodgings of M. de Lansac in the Rue St Honoré. Spared on account of his youth by order of the Count, the boy had been put in the charge of an officer of the guards, La Rochette. That man, seeing how glad his young prisoner was at hearing that one of his father's trusted followers had been saved, offered to go and fetch Mergey and bring him safely to the Rue St Honoré. 'M. de la Rochette,' wrote Mergey, 'came to my lodgings at the count's request and from the door of my room said to me in a gruff and threatening voice: "Come along, now!", not adding another word. Not knowing that he had been sent by the count, but being well aware that he was a great enemy of those of the Religion, I was expecting to go, not over, but under the Pont-aux-Meuniers, like so many others. I bowed very low, while he, in an even more threatening voice, said: "Come on! come on!" I then asked whether I was to take my sword, and he answered: "Who is going to attack you? Would you not defend yourself?" "Of course," I said, "and fight hard!"

'Then, softening his voice and laughing, he added: "Well, come along. Count de la Rochefoucauld wants you".

' I bowed again lower still and with great pleasure. And taking my sword and a halberd from one of his companions—he had six or seven of them and they had badly frightened me at first— we went out to find the Count; and when he saw me, he threw himself upon my neck and embraced me long, unable to speak, sobbing and sighing, and I did the same.'

A similar episode should be mentioned here, a strange one which sounded thoroughly miraculous to its hero, a M. de Regnier, from the neighbourhood of Montauban.[1]

Vezins, a Quercy gentleman, had been for a long time on very bad terms with his neighbour, Regnier, a Calvinist whose death he had sworn. Both were in Paris and Regnier was terrified lest Vezins should take the opportunity of satisfying his long hatred and take his life. While he was dreading such an issue, the door of his room was thrown open and Vezins entered holding his naked sword, accompanied by two soldiers. 'Follow me', he said to Regnier in a curt, harsh voice. The latter walked out between the soldiers in great dismay, certain that he was walking to his death. Vezins made him mount his horse and they rode quickly out of Paris. Without halting, in dead silence he took him to his own castle in Quercy and then said: 'Now you are safe. I could have taken this opportunity to avenge myself, but men of honour must share one another's danger. That is why I saved you. When you feel inclined, you can always find me ready to settle our quarrel like gentlemen.'

Regnier replied, protesting his gratitude and begging for his friendship. 'I leave you at liberty to love or to hate me,' answered Vezins. 'I brought you here merely to allow you to make

[1] Sully's *Memoirs*.

your choice.' Without waiting for an answer, he spurred his horse and rode off.[1]

It may be added that Vezins even left Regnier the horse he had lent him and would not agree to take it back.[2]

This fine display of generosity may not be unique, as has been suggested, but it was certainly exceptional.

At the close of a day marked by so many horrors and a very small number of commendable deeds, one is tempted to make an estimate of the number of the dead. But it is impossible. Though August 24, 1572, is rightly the date of the massacre, it was far from being the only day on which massacre took place. The orders of the King and Queen failed to restore peace to Paris and France simply by virtue of the trumpets sounded at the cross-roads. We recall the words in which the Town Clerk described the Provost's and aldermen's efforts: 'All through the night and the following days and nights.' We have now to deal with those days and nights, and the massacre which was to spread all over France as soon as the news from Paris reached other parts of the kingdom. According to Michelet, 'The St Bartholomew massacre was not a day but a season. They went on killing here and there all through September and October'. It is much too soon, therefore, to quote figures. Moreover, when the time comes, we shall find it very difficult to reach a reliable approximation.

[1] Anquetil, *L'Esprit de la ligue, ou Histoire politique des troubles en France aux XVIe et XVIIe siècles.*
[2] Dulaure, *Histoire de Paris.*

CHAPTER SIX

The Days and Nights
that Followed

ON the morning of the 25th, Charles IX rose and went at once to his open window, as he was wont to do: he did not shudder nor show any disgust at the sight that met his gaze, for the Louvre had not been cleared of the corpses that had been dragged there and piled up the day before. He simply felt glad of the promise of splendid weather. It was very early and from the Seine came a faint mist, still tinged with the reflections of the sunrise, foretelling an exceptionally fine day, warm but not sultry. This early morning well-being would expand into perfect good-humour when he heard the first news from the Provost: Paris had slept like an overfed beast and it seemed that at sunrise the rioting had not begun again.

The King could now calmly review the situation with his mother, his brothers and their councillors. Of course, he was not too pleased with Guise's attitude. But there was a chance that, by playing this dangerous game—pretending to disapprove of the massacre and apparently protecting Huguenots—the young Duke might harm his popularity in Paris.

The most important aspect of the question was that, by complying with royal orders, the city had shown itself obedient. At the very beginning of the meeting Coligny's name had been mentioned, for his successor as Lord Grand Admiral had had to be appointed. In spite of the Chevalier d'Angoulême's hopes, the Marquis de Villards was eventually selected. Several other appointments were made: Henri de Mesmes, Seigneur de Malassise, took Francourt's place as Chancellor to the King of Navarre, and Villequier, one of Anjou's favourites, secured Pruney's treasurership. Coligny's name was heard again: a

Continuation of the Dubois picture (opposite). Coligny's decapitated
body can be seen in the centre, with the Duc de Guise behind it.

De Moort van Parys gepleegt Anno 157[

Panorama of
massacre,
from an
engraving
in the
Cabinet des
Estampes.
(Studios
Josse
Lalance)

Continuation
overleaf

troop was sent to Chatillon-sur-Loing to seize his sons and nephews—his brother Dandelot's sons, whom he had adopted on their father's death. But when the King's men arrived at Chatillon the elder boys—those whom the King had most wanted brought back to Paris—had been warned in time and had escaped.

The Admiral's ghost hovered over the council again when Catherine, who until then had scarcely intervened, told them that she had the day before been given his secret papers, seized in the Rue de Bethisy.

The most important document was his will, written during the last days of the third religious war, just before the peace of 1570, when the Huguenots' position was so precarious that they expected the worst. In it Catherine had found a few sentences which she was going to use to enlighten those who might still regret his death, especially her own son Alençon, whom she was glad to humiliate in public.

'Look,' she said. 'Do you want to know the advice the King received from your good friend the Admiral, whom you liked and respected so much ?'

'I would be delighted.'

'Well, there is a long paragraph in his will to explain to the King that he must not give too much land or power to his brothers. What do you say to that ?'

Alençon did not hesitate to answer drily: 'I don't know how far the Admiral was my friend, but in truth he has shown by this piece of advice how much he loved the King.'

Catherine choked with wrath, but she could find nothing to say in reply. Her son's words did not prevent her from trying again during the days that followed to use Coligny's will on other people, with a similar lack of success.

Then for the moment she changed the subject. Ransacking the archives she had found a letter to William of Orange, dated June 15th, in which Coligny had written: 'We shall be ready by September'. She pretended to believe that it was proof of the Huguenot conspiracy which had never existed, as she knew better than anybody else. Certainly no member of the Council was taken in: all of them knew well that by June 15th Coligny was hoping to be successful in bringing French troops into Flanders, without the least need of conspiracy. Tavannes himself had written, more or less at the same date: 'Everything is in favour of the Huguenot plan and everything looks ready for the overthrow of the Spaniards.' It was perfectly normal that Coligny should have wished to reassure William of Orange and to take him into his confidence. But the Queen Mother's interpretation was useful in justifying the horrors of the previous day about which the councillors were undecided whether to boast or to make a defence. So the letter was put aside with a few other documents—very few—which might be useful.

Finally Anjou came along with more papers which had been found in Téligny's house, letters sent to the young man by the Marshal de Montmorency. Just after the attempted murder of the 22nd, the latter had written that he was ready to take his revenge as if the crime had been committed against his own person.

'If he thought like that after a mere wound,' added Anjou, 'you may guess what he thinks today, now that the Admiral is dead!'

Now what was essential was not an elaborate discussion about what had happened so much as to check its consequences. It was a good omen that quietness reigned over Paris.

The Miracle of the mayflower

What the King and his councillors were taking for a lasting calm was only a short-lived respite, which was just about to end. Everything started again because of a flower, a hawthorn which burst into bloom at noon in the Holy Innocents Churchyard. 'A dead and withered thorn shot forth green branches and fresh flowers'[1] in the middle of August. It was a miracle and the news spread through Paris like wildfire.

Had one cared to look closer, one might have noticed that the old Franciscan who watched over the churchyard had helped to bring about the miracle. But troops were sent at once and put on guard round the 'marvellous thorn', keeping people at a distance. Before Paris had time to think, preachers and monks were able to make use of the miracle without encountering scepticism.

A hawthorn blossoming out of season was the obvious manifestation of God's will: not only to approve what had been done, but to show that His wrath had been sated to encourage the Parisians to better deeds.

[1] Capilupi, De Stratagemi de Charles IX.

The mob flocked to the cemetery in a fantastic display of mysticism and superstition: sixteenth century Parisians were not very different from their tenth century ancestors and their faith was still loaded with the vestiges of ageless paganism. Monks went into hysterics, brandishing their crucifixes, women writhed and yelled: 'A miracle! A miracle!'. Groups of murderers reformed and gaily set out again on a new orgy of blood.

This began near the Rue de Béthisy, where Coligny's mangled remains had been exposed for more than twenty-four hours to the most revolting outrages, and a disgusting procession was organized to carry what was left of him to the gallows at Montfaucon. And after getting back into training by glutting their eyes on these fragments of human flesh, they felt a new craving to torture and sacrifice living victims.

The scenes which then took place were almost identical with those of the day before, which have already been fully described. It all started again, 'the roar of constant gunfire, the fearful screams of those who were butchered, the murderers' yells, the bodies that were thrown from the windows or dragged in the mud amidst shouts of rage and derision, the breaking of doors and windows, the stoning and looting of more than 600 houses'. It went on endlessly, and the archives of the City Hall show a large number of protests by the Court between the 25th and the 30th, all trying to re-establish peace and to stop the slaughter of Huguenots and the plundering of their houses.

On the 25th all the City's troops were called to arms, 'on horseback if possible, if not on foot'. On the 26th Robert Grisson, the Grand Provost's lieutenant, read a royal edict, the concluding sentence of which ran as follows: '. . . to be quite sure that no harm or unpleasantness be done to people of the religion, and that they should be well protected, under pain of death'.

On the 27th a new edict was issued: 'His Majesty, desiring that all murders and looting should cease, wills and commands that all the merchants and aldermen's provosts shall place a small guard of ten men at the end of each street with orders to prevent any killing, murdering or plundering.'

Two days later, on the 29th, the King, whose impotence had been demonstrated by the number and futility of his appeals, found means to shift his responsibilities on to other shoulders in a way which weak governments were to follow later. He appointed a committee of twelve members, of judges and city officials, so to 'arrange things that murders and looting shall cease'.

On the 30th this new City Council could do no more than publish this revealing notice: 'No harm shall be done to merchants and other foreigners living in houses and hostelries . . . or to Germans, to English, Flemish and other foreign students, who have simply taken refuge in various places.' And further on: 'See to it that all soldiers and archers who have entered houses shall leave without exacting any sort of ransom.'

After which, at the end of three or four days, during which the committee met only a few times, 'all the said members appointed by the King complained to him that it was inconvenient for them to sit and that there was little need for them to do so . . . after which the said assembly and commission ceased'.

Moreover, we must realize that the King finally accepted this lawless situation, for on September 5th, thirteen days after the fateful night, 'he sent for Pezou the butcher, one of the captains of Paris, and asked him whether there were still any Huguenots left in the city; to which Pezou replied that the day before he had thrown some six score into the water and there was about the same number due for the next night; at which the King laughed loudly and sent him away to see to his job'.

During the long troubled period heralded by the Miracle of the Mayflower, more supernatural events were reported: a statue of the Virgin wept and a new star shone in the sky. The list of victims grew longer each day, but it contained no more illustrious names. Indeed, most of the outstanding people had figured in the first lists and had been dispatched on the 24th by the King's men, or had been able that day to find refuge. Yet one may quote among the victims of the 'following days' a few great names which have already been mentioned: President La Place, La Force and his son Armand, and Ramus.

We may remember that La Place had been 'protected' in his own house by the city archers. On the 25th, 'two hours after dinner', Provost Seneçay arrived and ordered him to come to the King. As the magistrate was protesting, on account of the danger in the streets, where the massacre had broken out again, Seneçay gave him Pezou and ten of his archers as escort. This time, La Place knew what was in store for him. With great fortitude he raised his wife, who had thrown herself at the

Provost's feet, tore from his young son's hat the white cross the child had pinned there, hoping to save his life, and walked out to meet his death. He found it at the corner of the street, and while his murderers were hacking him to pieces the archers returned to his house to loot it.

When the King heard of the death of La Place, he merely published the name of the new President of the Cour des Aides whom he had already chosen: M. de Nully, of whom it may be said that his qualities so far had not brought him any notoriety.

As for La Force and his sons, their ransom had to be paid to Martin by Tuesday the 26th at the latest. But M. de Larchant had not abandoned hope of getting rid of his wife's half-brothers and co-heirs. So, during the afternoon of the 26th, it was not Martin who called at the house in the Rue des Petits-Champs, but one of Larchant's friends, the Comte de Coconas with fifty soldiers. Coconas said he was to take the prisoners to the Louvre, on the orders not of the King, but of his brother Anjou. The same scene was repeated: scarcely had the wretched men and their escort reached the corner of the street when daggers were drawn. Armand was stabbed first, then his father, and then Jacques-Nompar, the youngest, who fell screaming: 'I am dead!'[1]

He was not dead, but he displayed an extraordinary presence of mind. For several hours he remained motionless, lying under the bodies of his father and brother, who were still writhing in the agony of death. When night had fallen, the umpire of a tennis-court who was out to rob the corpses, noticed that the child was not dead and not even wounded. He took pity on him and helped him to reach the Arsenal where Marshal de Biron welcomed and protected him. The child who survived the St Bartholomew massacre lived to become a Marshal of France, a Duke and a Peer of the Realm, dying at ninety-four while Louis XIV was on the throne, the fifth of the Kings 'of whom he was alternatively the enemy and the servant'.[2]

Ramus, after having escaped the murderers whom Charpentier had sent on the Sunday to the Collège des Presles, did not stay even twenty-four hours in the cellar in the Rue Jean de

[1] Their page was saved by one of the Swiss.
[2] Duc de la Force, *Le Maréchal de la Force*. He was one of Henri IV's staunch followers, though he remained a firm Protestant all his life. His first wife was Marshal de Biron's daughter.

Beauvais, where his students had made him hide. On Tuesday, thinking he had probably gone back to his garret—or warned perhaps by an informer—the assassins returned to the Rue des Carmes, climbed to the fifth floor and, finding the philosopher at his prayers like Coligny, with the door not even locked, they stabbed him three or four times and threw his body out of the window. Some students, intent to please Charpentier, made haste to drag his corpse to the Seine, scourging it all the way.

An argument against premeditation

So far, only Paris has been mentioned, but it is high time to see what took place in the provinces and to enquire into the repercussions and sequels of the Paris matins in the principal towns and the countryside. It was, indeed, only a question of 'repercussions' and 'sequels', a fact that is of great significance.

In fact, there is no trace of any action, no matter how small, which can be said to have corresponded, with even the minimum of synchronism, with the actions launched against Protestants in Paris on the 24th. On the contrary, all those who might have known best were completely staggered by the news of the events in the capital. And everywhere where the example was to be followed disorder did not break out until after the arrival of messengers bearing despatches that told of the massacre of the Huguenots. It is enough to add that the delays were considerable, because of the distances involved and the slow means of communication. This also accounts for the fact that the most distant provincial cities—in the South, for instance—only heard of it some days later than certain foreign capitals nearer Paris, like Brussels or London. It is all the more interesting as it helps to throw some light on a much discussed aspect of the question, namely premeditation.

During the years that followed the St Bartholomew massacre, no one ever doubted such premeditation; Protestants and Catholics were completely agreed on this point at any rate. Among the latter, Capilupi for one, praised the Queen Mother's and her son's cunning and dissembling, while the Protestants denounced their disloyalty and duplicity.

But this unanimity lacked a solid historical basis on either side, and it did not last long. Subsequent discussions in which the Protestants were for premeditation and the Catholics against, had no good authority either.

There is a new and important proof against premeditation in the complete calm that reigned throughout Provincial France all through August 24th. Nothing would have been easier for Catherine, the King or the Guises, to send messengers to the main cities in good time to give orders for a massacre to be carried out on the day in question. That could certainly have been done, had not the council held on the night of the 23rd been a hasty improvisation, brought about by Maurevert's clumsiness and the attitude of the King.

This complete lack of synchronization not only provides evidence against premeditation; it also underlines how unlikely was Catherine's one attempt to give warning of the massacre, at the same time organizing military operations against the Huguenots. This strange document was a sealed letter which the Queen Mother was said to have sent, a few weeks earlier, to Colonel General Strozzi, who was at Brouage[1] with troops and a fleet. His presence there made the Spaniards as restless as the Protestants, as everybody knew that, in Coligny's mind and in the King's, those forces were intended to invade Flanders. Tavannes knew it well. Strozzi was the Queen's cousin. He received a mysterious letter which he was not to open until August 24th, and here is its content:

'Strozzi, I give you warning that today, August 24th, the Admiral and all the Huguenots who were here have been killed. Hence act at once to make yourself master of La Rochelle and do to the Huguenots who fall into your hands what we have done here. Be careful not to fail us, or dread the King my son's displeasure as well as mine.

Catherine.'

The original of the letter has never been found and it may be a forgery. It also may have been written on the 24th: there is nothing in the text to the contrary and that would account for the word 'today'. But it is quite unlikely that it was written weeks, or even days before the 24th: had it depended upon the Queen, Coligny would have been killed on the 22nd and not two days later. It would be even more unlikely as Strozzi, who had important forces at his disposal, took no action against La Rochelle on the 24th; also because if the Queen thought she

[1] A few miles south of La Rochelle.

could send such an order to Strozzi in a sealed letter without risk of its being intercepted, she might have done the same with other governors or partisans on whom she could rely in other provincial towns—in Meaux, for instance, where she was a countess in her own right.

At Meaux, which is very near Paris, her messengers arrived on Sunday afternoon and they saw the Queen's trusted agent, Procurator Louis Cosset. But the slaughter only began there at dawn on Monday. Elsewhere, the first messengers did not arrive before Monday. The furthest place reached on Monday night by the King's envoys seems to have been La Charité-sur-Loire, where Nevers' Italian companies were garrisoned, and they started work at once.

On each successive day the circle round Paris widened. One witness mentioned the fact that on Saturday the 30th a King's messenger passed Montpellier, bearing news of the St Bartholomew massacre.[1]

Full praise or full shame . . .

While messengers were riding post-haste along the main roads to carry the news throughout the kingdom from the Pyrenees to Picardy, from the Alps to Gascony, Provence and Normandy, the August blood-letting was continuing in Paris and the King had to make important political decisions.

One may recall the first letters he sent on the 24th, in which provincial governors were told of the Admiral's death and of the 'lamentable rebellion' resulting from a private quarrel between the Guises and the Chatillons. Three new facts emerged after they had been written. Guise had changed his attitude, wanting to shift the responsibility and compel the King to take his share of it; the enthusiasm of the Catholic party in Paris, which foretold an equally favourable attitude in the Catholic provinces; finally, the ease with which the tale of a Huguenot conspiracy had been swallowed. These three factors were so many arguments likely to bear upon the King's and his mother's decision: it was no longer necessary to give credit to others for such a popular enterprise. So Charles IX was going to commit himself utterly. On the 26th, after having heard mass as usual, he went in full ceremony to the 'gilded hall', where the whole Parliament was assembled, and held a bed of justice. His very first words,

[1] Philippi, *Mémoires*.

uttered in a solemn voice, claimed full responsibility for the crime: 'All that has happened in Paris has been done not only with my permission, but under my special command and on my own initiative. Consequently, I claim full praise or full shame for myself.'

The King knew well that no one in the audience would dare to speak of shame. Moreover, he had his motives: 'The rebellious and seditious Huguenots,' he went on, 'not content with having insulted His Divine Majesty, His churches and priests, or committing crimes for which we had forgiven them, dared to conspire against my own person and those of my blood. Knowing that I could only punish them through the means I have taken, I used them, and the idea may, since it has been successful, have been put into my heart by His Divine Majesty. . . .'

He concluded his speech by requesting the members of his Parliament to try the Admiral in effigy—as every other way was now out of the question—and also his accomplices who could be caught.

After him, de Thou, the First President, with a cowardice that his son vainly tried to diminish, made servile homage to the King, using for him a phrase which may have been formerly coined for Louis XI: 'Who cannot dissemble cannot reign'.[1]

Upheld by Parliament and approved by the Sorbonne, the King, two days later, in solemn procession, received the Church's tokens of gratitude. He was basking in his triumph and he almost believed that he was the equal of the conqueror of Lepanto and the true follower of Catherine in her cunning political line. He ordered Favier, 'General of the Mint', to send him drawings for commemorative medals. They were to be struck with his effigy and the date August 24, 1572, and the motto: 'Charles IX, Conqueror of the Rebels'.

But in order to gain complete victory he busied himself with what was going on in the provinces. Duplicity was certainly yielding good results, so the King was going beyond his mother's suggestions and was concocting a diabolical plan which involved the writing of innumerable letters, orders and edicts, very often contradicted by the verbal orders carried by trusted messengers. Thus, on August 27th, the day after the bed of justice, a letter was despatched to every provincial governor. They were not all

[1] J. A. de Thou, *Mémoires*.

alike. They took account of the outlook, known or assumed, of the receiver. Thus the officials of Bourges received the following message: 'We request and most strongly order that no trouble shall take place among the inhabitants of your city, nor any massacre be committed.' On the other hand, d'Orthe, Governor of Bayonne, who was a good Catholic but a compassionate man, was told that: 'It is to be feared some people, under this pretext, may take an opportunity to take revenge, for which I should be incredibly sorry.'

To all and sundry the King stated that he intended to maintain the Edict of Pacification. But at the same time his secret messengers were carrying other orders. They were as clear as they were pitiless: to take no account of the letters received, but to follow at once the example of Paris. Sorbin, the King's preacher, carried them to Orleans; Comartin and St Ritan carried them to Dijon, written by the King himself;[1] La Mole to the Comte de Tende, Governor of Provence, and Mareuil to Bourges.

On the 28th the King made a new public pretence of maintaining the Edict, saying that he would try the Huguenots who had held commands or who had been party to Coligny's conspiracy. In his declaration the King reiterated all he had already said in Parliament, claiming full responsibility.

Other letters penned on the 30th are rather surprising. Not realizing that he thereby admitted that he had sent out secret verbal orders, Charles wrote to Madelot, the Governor of Lyons: 'Whatever we may have ordered through those whom we sent out, when with all justification we feared some sinister event, we have cancelled and are cancelling all, and neither you nor others shall do any such thing'.

The whole process, one will agree, was a mixture of duplicity and naïve stupidity, apparent incoherency and very real baseness, which can be only explained as the result of the shock produced by the events of the 24th on an already tottering mind. Anyway, the consequences of such a startling succession of orders and counter-orders would be interesting to know.

The turn of the provinces

In all the provincial towns which followed the example of Paris, the same sequence of facts is to be observed. As soon as they

[1] President Jeannin, *Mémoires*.

had received the letters and instructions of August 24th, the governors took steps to ensure safety: the gates were closed, and Protestants were in many cases put under preventive arrest, and it was only after a few hours, or a few days, or sometimes a few weeks, that the secret orders were carried out, if at all.

That explains why, contrary to what happened in Paris, the wholesale massacre of Protestants in the Provinces took place most often in the prisons and not in the homes of the Huguenots; and these killings were usually the work of a few small groups, the population taking scarcely any share in them.

That is what happened in Meaux, for instance. Procurator Cosset and his men began on Tuesday evening to read a roll-call of Protestant prisoners at the top of the prison staircase. During several evenings in succession, between nine and twelve, after getting thoroughly drunk, they amused themselves by stabbing the wretched victims or clubbing them with cleavers borrowed from the slaughter house, and tumbling them down the steps. Thus in batches of twenty-five or thirty, 200 Huguenots had been dispatched within a few days.

Similarly in Troyes, the first orders arrived on the 26th and the first week was spent in filling the prisons. Then, on September 3rd, a messenger came from Paris with the King's orders to release the prisoners and all at once . . . and then further orders asking the Bailiff, Anne de Vaudrey, not to publish those letters until after the leading Huguenots had been duly slaughtered. The town hangman flatly refused to carry out the task, and it was done by a sergeant, Pernet, with the help of the gaolers and a few unsavoury gaolbirds. On September 5th, Anne de Vaudrey, 'using the medicine after the death', had the King's letters and declarations of the 28th and 30th read throughout the town to the accompaniment of trumpets, purporting to 'prohibit the massacre, plundering, looting or arrest of any members of the religion'.[1]

In Orleans the massacre took place as soon as the King's preacher and confessor, Arnaud Sorbin, had brought the Court's secret orders, although forty-eight hours late. It was done more or less after the Paris fashion, and the mob, led by a few captains, gaily took part in the slaughter and looting for about a week. According to the killers themselves, some 1,200 Huguenots were murdered and their bodies thrown into the

[1] Simon Goulart.

Loire. Many cases can be cited of atrocities fully equal to those that had taken place in Paris.

In Bourges the massacre started on the 27th at dawn: it was brought about by news from Orleans, together with orders brought from Paris by a messenger who had been sent there to inquire what was to be done, when the attack of August 22nd had been reported. The town officials received the royal orders a little later. They had the effect of re-establishing order for a few days. They were brought by the same messenger, Mareuil, who, on his return, told how different were the court's secret intentions from the orders officially transmitted. So that, after two or three days, the Protestants who had been set free and who thought they were safe, were rearrested and thrown into prison, and on September 11th, shortly before midnight, the murderers, led by the city captains, methodically assassinated them all.

In Lyons, during the last days of August, the same process of order and counter-order brought about the same result. The Governor of this city, the second in the kingdom, had for one year been a M. de Mandelot, successor to the Duke de Nemours, which itself was proof of the great importance of his office. On the morning of the 27th, Mandelot received a letter from the King, telling him of the first disorders in Paris. This letter, which laid the blame on the Guises, showed that the King was going to have justice done.

As a precaution, and possibly to prevent the Protestants from being molested by unruly Catholics, the Governor had the gates closed and patrols of arquebusiers sent through the streets. Actually, the first attacks were made upon the persons and the property of the Huguenots during the night of the 27th, but they were few and widely scattered. Secret messages arrived from Paris during the two following days. Two aldermen, de Masso and Scarro, and Procurator Claude de Rubis who had been sent to the Court to ask what was to be done against the Huguenots, sent back an account of the events of the 24th, adding that the King had declared and commanded them to let the Lyons Consuls know that 'His Majesty's intention is to see them do as Paris has done'. Yet, on the other hand, another Lyonnais, Maurice de Payrat, came back from Paris, bringing to Mandelot another letter from the King (the one dated the 24th), stating the official position: 'Nothing should be done to break the Edict of Pacification . . . and I beg you to see that everyone can live in peace and safety in his own house.' What was Mandelot to do?

His hesitation merely reflects the contradictory orders he had received. On the Saturday he summoned the city officials and made the militia responsible for the Huguenots' lives and possessions. The next day, he had all the Huguenots summoned by the herald and brought to the Governor's house to hear the King's will. Most of them, trusting in the King's word, obeyed the summons. They were immediately arrested and sent to various monasteries, to the Roanne prison and even to the Archbishop's palace. And on Monday, while Mandelot was investigating a rebellion which was supposed to have broken out at La Guillotière, armed bands rushed to the assault of the improvised prisons, broke down the gates without difficulty and slaughtered all the Huguenot prisoners, among whom was the great musician Goudimel.[1] For several days the killing and looting went on and the Rhone carried down so many fearfully mangled bodies that, as far as Provence, people living along the river preserved that hideous memory and refused to drink the water for a long time.

So far it had only been a question of a few regions in which, with varying delays, Huguenots had been executed as a direct consequence of news received from Paris. Even in Lyons and Bourges the massacres were perpetrated in the heat of the moment, as the mass excitement caused by the shock of the events of August 24th had not really calmed down.

It was the same in a few other towns, mostly in Touraine and Anjou: Blois, Tours, Saumur, Angers and Beaupréau, where the killers, led by M. de Montsoreau, began their work on the 26th on orders received from Montpensier and Puygaillard.

It is more surprising to see the reactions of other big provincial cities where feelings after the 24th had been less strong, where the peace had been scarcely disturbed and quickly became total once more, and where in the middle of September or even early in October, the massacre suddenly broke out, this time in cold blood and as violently as anywhere else. This happened in Rouen, where the Governor, de Carouges, ignored the King's secret orders, so that he was harshly blamed by the Court. Those

[1] Among other things, he had set Marot's translation of the Psalms to music.

orders were repeated rather impatiently, and sent to a few people in Rouen well-known for their hatred of the Huguenots. The vicar of St Pierre, Claude Mortereul, and a Captain Laurent de Maromme, seized the opportunity of a day when the Governor was out of town. Leading a gang of rioters, they had the prison gates opened and began by killing some sixty Protestants whom Carouges thought he had protected by locking them up. Afterwards the gang broke loose into the city and perpetrated what has already been so often described.

That happened on September 18th. Two days later, seven Protestants were murdered in the prisons of Roanne, and much later, on October 2nd and 3rd, similar scenes were repeated in Toulouse and Bordeaux.

We can stop at this point: these were the most important cities and towns in which the homicidal fury of the Court and of Paris found dutiful followers.

The King's orders resisted

Let us now go back to the day following St Bartholomew and start again round France, stopping this time at places where resistance to the King's orders, put up by governors, aldermen, officers and sometimes even by Roman Catholic priests, succeeded in saving the Protestants. These were not isolated cases: if one marks on a map of France in 1572 the cities and districts in which Protestants were massacred between August and October it will be seen that they far from cover the larger part of the kingdom or the majority of cities.

This can be credited first to the humane and courageous attitude of certain provincial governors, who ran the risk of the King's anger, and that of the Queen Mother and other powerful persons at Court. On this roll of honour one may inscribe the names of the Comte de Tende (Governor of Provence), Gordes (in the Dauphiny), St Herem (in Auvergne), Longueville (in Picardy), and beyond the Alps, Ludovic de Birague in the Marquisate of Saluces, which had been French for twenty-five years and was to remain so for fifteen more.

The fact should also be recorded that in some towns where many Huguenots were killed, this was against the will and orders of the provincial Governor: such was the case in Rouen, Toulouse and Troyes, which were practically the only cities in Normandy, Languedoc or Champagne in which, on the initiative of the local authorities, or of irresponsible agitators, the governors' orders were transgressèd. Those governors were Matignon, Damville and, strange to say, Guise himself!

One must add Britanny and Burgundy to the list of provinces preserved or partially preserved from massacres. The Governor of Burgundy was the Duke d'Aumale, though it was in fact administered by a lieutenant-general, Chabot-Charny. In Britanny, if the Governor had had a free hand things would have been worse than elsewhere, as this was Montpensier. It happened that Montpensier was kept at Court, but as from the morrow of the St Bartholomew's day he sent violent orders to every part of his region. But the civil and military authorities alike, the aldermen of Nantes and the troops commanded by Bouillé, flatly refused to obey. The Nantes aldermen were not the only ones who succeeded in compelling their towns to respect the lives and properties of the Huguenots whatever Paris or the capital of the province had ordered. In Limoges, the local consuls took the same measures to avoid all violence, and one might mention many other examples.

Elsewhere, it was simply the governor's attitude which tipped the scales. Orthe in Bayonne, Glandage in Die, Bories in Périgueux, de Guiche in Mâcon, and Sigogne in Dieppe succeeded in saving the Protestants, sometimes by locking them up for a few days or a few weeks to protect them from fanatical Catholics. They kept their own names and that of their cities free from stain. Even a few high dignitaries of the Catholic church, like Archbishop Grimaldi of Vienne, displayed humanity and tolerance, protecting and even sheltering the Huguenots.

Such resistance to the King's orders by men like Orthe, Tende or St Herem, who had displayed outstanding cruelty in former conflicts, did not pass without a few incidents here and there. Some of them should be recorded, in so far as they throw light on the behaviour of the King, his mother and the secret council. Let us take three instances: Burgundy, Provence and Normandy.

It has already been said that two messengers arrived at Dijon on the 26th with letters from the King, and that they had to deliver a verbal message to Comte de Chabot-Charny, Lieutenant-General and Grand Equery of France, to the effect that the Protestants of Dijon were to be dealt with as those of Paris had been. Chabot-Charny called his councillors together. One of them, the lawyer Jeannin,[1] thought of a stratagem: he suggested that the King's two messengers should be heard separately and that they should notify the council in writing and under their own signatures of the orders they were carrying. Of course, they both refused to sign, fearing to be held responsible for the slaughter and to be disowned later by the King.

'On their refusal,' wrote Jeannin, 'I quoted the law of the Emperor Theodosius who, after having in a fit of anger ordered the death of a great number of Christians, was ejected from the Christian community by St Ambrosius, who forced him to make penance and to promulgate a new law to atone for his sin, by which all Governors who should receive such extraordinary orders should wait thirty days, during which they should send to the Emperor to have a new order penned in due form.' At Jeannin's suggestion, the council resolved to send a messenger to the King—without much hurry, as there was plenty of time— to inquire whether he was still of the same mind, and if so, to secure letters patent, signed in his own hand.

The Governor of Provence, the Comte de Tende, had also received a Court messenger a few days after the St Bartholomew massacre. The man was a nobleman from Arles, La Mole, who was in Alençon's retinue. He brought letters from the secret council with orders to massacre all the Huguenots in Provence. Having read the letter, Tende is reported to have remarked that such orders could not come from the King who, in an earlier message, blamed the Guises for the massacre in Paris, adding: 'I think there are some who usurp Royal authority to glut their passions. Consequently, I shall obey the first letters, as they agree better with the royal majesty. As for this new message you bring, it is so barbarous and cruel that, even if the King in person had bid me obey, I would not do so.'

His courageous attitude was not without great risk, and 'shortly afterwards, the Governor of Avignon was poisoned and his office given to the Comte de Retz, the Queen Mother's principal favourite'.

As for Matignon, the Governor of Normandy who also strove to protect the Protestants, he took the initiative, doubtless to

---

[1] Pierre Jeannin (1540-1622), born in Autun, one of the outstanding lawyers of his time. He was mostly in opposition to the Guises, though he served the League some time, in order to try to give it some legal background. Then he went over to Henri IV and was among the lawyers who drafted the Edict of Nantes. He met James I's envoys in Holland in 1607.

protect himself, of having the King's official despatches printed and distributed like handbills: they all confirmed liberty of thought, maintained the Edict of Pacification, and ordered the protection of Protestants. It is true that Charles IX had seen that those orders alone had been given in writing and signed by him. But this was only in order that, later on, he could disown responsibility for the massacre, and not so that the Governors, taking refuge in his authority, might restrain Catholic enthusiasm.

Anne de Vaudrey at Troyes, for instance, understood the King's scheme very well, when he had the edicts read all over the town after all the Huguenots had been killed. Matignon, on the other hand, simply refused to understand, and Charles IX told him what he thought of him in a furious note:[1] 'I think it is marvellously strange that, instead of keeping them secret and unpublished, you allow the letters and dispatches I sent you after the Admiral's death to be printed and divulged everywhere.' And after having admitted that he dreaded that the letters should be sent out of the kingdom, he ordered Matignon to burn all the copies he could lay his hand on, and 'have the type taken away from the press at once, and privately, so that, by making amends for this blunder, a greater one is not made'.

A traitor to his own soldiers

The Duke of Longueville, Governor of Picardy, was one of those whose brave attitude succeeded in saving his province from the murderous infection. He proved so scrupulous in his attempt to keep order and quiet that, writing to d'Humières, the Governor of Péronnes, at the end of August, he reproached him for having allowed the Catholics to loot a Protestant church. On September 22nd, he complained to the King of the repercussions which the sinister exploits of Captain de Maromme and his Rouen gang might have in Picardy. Yet the same Longueville was closely associated with a crime of first magnitude, which was a direct consequence of the St Bartholomew massacre and which perhaps surpasses, if not in horror, at least in baseness, all that has been related hitherto.

It will not have been forgotten that, at Coligny's urgent request, and also on the King's orders, a number of French soldiers, all of them Protestants, had been sent to Flanders

[1] Quoted by H. de la Ferrière, *La St Barthélemy*.

under de Genlis to fight the Spanish troops of the Duke óf Alva along with William of Orange's 'Beggars'. After Genlis' defeat before Mons in July, the survivors of the expeditionary forces were either Alva's prisoners with Genlis, or had shut themselves up with Louis of Nassau in Mons, which they defended with the courage of despair, to the admiration of their enemies.

Those Frenchmen, badly engaged and already terribly mauled, were to provide Charles IX with an opportunity to commit the worst treason imaginable: that of a sovereign and army chief who betrays his own men to the enemy and finally has them massacred.

On August 31st Charles wrote to Mondoucet, his representative in Brussels: 'The Duke of Alva has with him several of my rebellious subjects and the means to take Mons and punish those who are inside. If he does not do so, I shall have great reason to complain and to blame him for all the evil which may result. If he says to you that it means tacitly to kill the aforesaid prisoners and cut to pieces those inside Mons, you will reply that that is what he must do.'[1] A week later, he sent another letter to confirm these instructions, marvelling at the fact that his orders had not been carried out.

In fact, Mondoucet had been horrified by what he was asked to do. For his own part, Alva, who was certainly not renowned in Flanders for his generosity, had resolved not to render the King of France the 'service' the latter had demeaned himself to ask for. On the contrary, while being very pleased with the St Bartholomew massacre and its value to Spain, he wanted Charles IX and France to bear alone all the odium which would fall on them sooner or later. The pitiless, bloodthirsty Alva did what he had never done before: he made a treaty with the defenders of Mons, granted them the honours of war, bowed to their ensigns and let them go free.

Then Longueville stepped in. On September 18th, Charles wrote to him: 'My cousin, I have already written to you that there was some talk that the Duke of Alva would come to terms with those of Mons and set free my subjects whom he took when Genlis was defeated, sending them back to my kingdom. I have told you to take heed and not suffer such rebels to return, but to pursue them. . . .'

Again, quoting more rumours about the imminent surrender

[1] Quoted by H. de la Ferrière.

of Mons and the fact that the garrison was to be set free, he added: 'I wanted to have you warned to be ready to march upon them and give them the welcome that I have already written to you.'

On the 27th, Longueville sent his report: he had, in fact, given the men of Mons the welcome the King desired. Five or six hundred foot soldiers, marching towards Guise and La Cappelle, had been cut to pieces, with the exception of some 100 or 120, whom Rothelin was pursuing and hoped to liquidate. It had been more difficult with cavalry but by groups of twenty or thirty they had been pursued and cut down. . . .

World opinion

When an event of first magnitude occurs and we of the second half of the twentieth century wish to discover how the capitals of the world have reacted to it, we naturally consult the newspapers of different opinions, because they are more or less the mirror of public opinion. We may also examine diplomatic reports, or remarks uttered by public or private people in proportion to their importance. This multiplicity of sources may enable us to gauge the importance of the event and sometimes to prophesy what it may lead to.

When there are no newspapers and no genuine expression of public opinion, we can only take into account the reaction of governments seen from two viewpoints: those to be found in the various national archives and those of which French diplomats made themselves the interpreters and which are to be found in the French archives. As for the opinions expressed by important people other than reigning sovereigns, they do not amount to much, as they could only have been brought together in sufficient number by a modern newspaper system. These reservations are necessary to explain the very limited nature of the reactions to the news of the St Bartholomew massacre. They are the reactions of sovereigns rather than of peoples or even of ruling classes.

Let us consult first the documents from Rome: obviously it was there that the event would rouse the greatest interest. It was regarded as one of the main episodes of the wars of religion and very probably as their ultimate phase.

As early as September 2nd, thanks to a horseman sent post-haste from Lyons by Governor Mandelot, Rome knew roughly what had happened on August 24th: the Admiral was dead, together with most of the Huguenot lords living in Paris or there for Navarre's wedding, and the King's will was that the same should be done throughout the provinces.

Gregory XIII was so pleased by the news that he granted one hundred crowns to the messenger. But he waited for official confirmation before rejoicing. The Seigneur de Beauville was sent by the French court to fulfil that pleasant duty. On September 5th he appeared before the Pope, who was surrounded by the Cardinals, and delivered a letter from the King, requesting the Holy Father to believe what he was about to be told.

Beauville also brought a message from the Nuncio Salviati, and a letter from Montpensier, expressing joy at the thought that 'it has pleased God to enlighten the King who had done execution on the Admiral and his accomplices', and finally a detailed and circumstantial note from the Cardinal de Bourbon, insisting on the official version of the massacre: 'The Admiral had conspired to have the King, his mother and brothers and all the Catholic princes and lords in their suite killed, and that being done, to set up a King of his own faith; and to abolish all religion in the kingdom but his own.'[1] The Ambassador Extraordinary, as we have seen, had left Paris on the 26th. Had he left twenty-four hours earlier, he would of course have told the Pope of the 'detestable rebellion caused by the old quarrel between the Guises and the Chatillons'. . . .

Thus the Pope first knew of the events through a very vague story. That may account in part for his immediate reactions. For in the Vatican archives there is a record of the speech in which he replied to the French King's envoy. This fragment, which deserves to be quoted in full, reflects complete satisfaction, without any afterthought: '. . . Charles has also displayed before our Most Holy Master and this entire assembly the most splendid virtues which can shine in the exercise of power. Let us thank him as a man; let us congratulate him in the name of the Church of God and His Holiness for having shown how far friendship can go. . . . Charles has resumed the old traditional fight for the Christian religion. No King could offer anything of greater value, worthy at the same time of his own glory and the virtues of his ancestors'. And the speech continued in this way, with a mass of compliments and superlatives.

[1] Quoted by de Meaux.

Pierre Champion has written: 'Rome was not to remain long in this illusion. Charles IX, made to look great in their eyes for a moment because of an act perpetrated in tumult and muddle, for which he had been wrongly given the credit and of which he had boasted in order to glorify himself, was soon to be better known for what he was, infantile and incoherent.'[1]

A very clever and true statement, which rectifies certain too indulgent judgments on the attitude of Gregory XIII to the St Bartholomew massacre. It is true that the Pope had not believed in Charles for a long time—or in Catherine, whose diplomats, after the slaughter of the Huguenots, continued contact with the heretical courts and even the infidels. But it does not mean that the Pope either condemned or regretted the fearful execution made in the name of the faith.

Vasari's paintings, which still decorate the walls of the Sala Regia in the Vatican; the medal struck at the order of the Pope, with his own profile on the face, and on the back the angel of doom cleaving the Protestants; the salvoes fired from the Castel St Angelo; and finally the decision to commemorate on September 11th the joint anniversaries of Lepanto and St Bartholomew—all these are so many proofs of persistent pontifical pleasure.

Of course, the Cardinal of Lorraine was in Rome and he spent himself and his money making the most of the situation. He organized a thanksgiving mass on September 8th in the Church of St Louis of the French, and when Gregory XIII walked between the rows of pontifical guards, he could read a grandoise inscription in gold letters, associating his own name with that of the Most Christian King, who 'suddenly, like an avenging angel divinely sent, had, by certain means, practically exterminated all the heretics in his kingdom'.

Madrid's pleasure was equal to that of Rome. On September 7th, Jean de Oleagni arrived with the news. He was secretary to His Catholic Majesty's Ambassador in Paris. Oleagni had started on his journey on Sunday afternoon. Philip II, when he broke the seal of the dispatch, could relish a first hand account of the events, which had a certain similarity to modern journalism:

'While I am writing, they are being killed everywhere,' wrote the Ambassador. 'They are stripped and dragged through the

---

[1] *Charles IX, la France et le contrôle de l'Espagne après la St Barthélemy.*
The answer to the Envoy Extraordinary Beauville is also taken from this book.

streets; houses are looted and no children spared. Praise be to God who has converted the French princes to His cause! May He inspire them to continue as they have begun!'[1]

The King of Spain went at once to a *Te Deum* in the monastery of San Geronimo. Then he gave an interview to Charles IX's Ambassador, St Gouard, and they congratulated each other. It is a fact that Spain could not have won a greater victory, either on land or at sea, a fact which St Gouard did not fail to stress in a sentence which has defied time, possibly on account of its bad taste:

'Admit, Sire, that you owe the Netherlands to the King my master!'

Throughout the next few days messengers continued to arrive from France, bringing all sorts of documents: the letters from Cuniga, who cleverly underlined the almost casual aspect of the massacre, started by a misfired shot, letters from Catherine to her former son-in-law, and an account by Don Diego of the audiences granted him by the Queen Mother on the 30th and by the King on the 31st, in which Charles did not fail to demand the slaughter of his own soldiers in Flanders.

On October 11th, at last, His Catholic Majesty gave his instructions to Don Antonio de Gusman, Marques de Ayamonte, whom he was sending as Envoy Extraordinary to the French King to congratulate him, as well as the Queen Mother and Anjou: 'Tell the Most Christian King,' added Philip, 'that as brother to brother, I most earnestly request him to continue what has been so well begun and so to punish rebellious Huguenots that they and their false doctrine are wiped for ever from the face of his kingdom.'[2]

Yet we must confess that, apart from Rome and Madrid, European capitals were far from being pleased with the French royal family and their advisers.

In England, the Ambassador, La Mothe-Fénelon, had to wait for eleven days before Queen Elizabeth granted him an interview, and the unusual ceremonial shown for his visit says much for the Queen's state of mind. She was in full mourning. She was attended by her whole court, and when the Ambassador entered he was greeted by deathly silence. Having nothing better to say, he told the story of the conspiracy against the

---

[1] Quoted by H. de la Ferrière.
[2] Quoted by de Meaux.

King and his family, but he knew all the time that the Queen could not be taken in. Besides, several of the Huguenots who had escaped from the Faubourg St Germain—Montgomery, the Vidame de Chartres and others—were already in England; their tale had been much more credible—and was actually believed—than his own laborious explanations.

He knew, too, that Walsingham, the English Ambassador in Paris, had also sent in his report, which not only recorded what he had seen, but also commented upon the various changes in the official version, together with an account of what the Queen Mother had told him.

Walsingham was one of those on whom Catherine had tried to use Coligny's political testament as a means of soiling the Admiral's memory. The trick had already failed with Alençon and it failed again with the Ambassador.

'Do you know,' she had said, 'that the Admiral advised the King my son to be suspicious always of the power of the English.'

Walsingham answered more or less like Alençon:

'He certainly had no liking for England. But in that respect he showed himself a loyal servant of the French Crown.'

And, without allowing her time to answer, the Ambassador went on to demand that reparations should be made for the murder of three Englishmen by the rioters in the Latin Quarter.

From Germany, Schomberg also wrote about the disastrous effect on the Princes of the massacre of the Huguenots, and he made himself felt to the extent that the Queen thought herself obliged to write to him: 'Do not think that what has been done to the Admiral and his accomplices was done out of hatred for the new religion, or to eradicate it, but merely to punish the dastardly conspiracy they had made.'

Gantrie, the French Envoy to the Swiss Cantons, wrote to Catherine that 'he would never dare to report' what he had heard about her and her son. Montluc and Choisnin, who were canvassing on Anjou's behalf for the vacant throne of Poland, were at their wits' end: 'Someone suddenly turned up, bringing the disastrous news, enriched with so many details that in a few hours the name of France was detested by most persons.'[1]

'Disastrous news'! A phrase which must have sounded very discordant in Paris in September 1572.

[1] Choisnin, *Mémoires*.

Of course, England, Germany, Switzerland and even part of Poland were under some Protestant influence or other: Anglican, Calvinist or Lutheran. But there was another capital, where the reaction was such that it deserves special mention; this was Vienna where Charles IX's father-in-law, the Holy Roman Emperor Maximilian, reigned. He heard the news only on September 16th, through his Ambassador Vulcob. The King's father-in-law listened without interruption as the letters written by Charles to Vulcob on August 22nd and 28th were read; they had arrived at the Embassy together. Then he delivered judgment: 'I know that it is not my son-in-law who governs. But that is not enough to pardon him. Had he asked my advice, he would not now be soiled by a stain he will never be able to wipe away.'[1]

The Princes' conversion

During the days and weeks which followed St Bartholomew's Day, while the King and the Catholic lords went in procession to the bed of justice, and while foreign capitals rang with the *Te Deum* or registered their indignation at the news of the massacre, what had happened to the Huguenots who had escaped the slaughter?

The two young princes, Henri de Navarre and Henri de Condé, spared by the express decision of the council, were kept imprisoned in the King's apartments, where they were safe, while quite close to them their most trusted friends and servants fell to the murderers' blows.

Charles, who had given them the choice between mass or death, expected to be able to publicize their conversion as one more victory of the Faith, and above all, as a justification of the crime. But both princes held out and delayed the fateful moment with all the resourcefulness they could muster, Navarre with his cunning and suppleness, Condé with straightforward obstinacy.

A former pastor of the reformed religion, who had recanted to save his life and liberty, Hugues Sureau, called du Rosier, had been selected to indoctrinate Navarre and his sister, and also the Prince and Princess de Condé.[2] As might be expected, he had no great difficulty in convincing Navarre and the two

---

[1] Theiner, *Annales ecclesiastici.*
[2] Sureau eventually repented and went back to Protestantism.

princesses.[1] Navarre, it seems, simply wanted to be able to say later that he had only given way under compulsion. 'Compulsion' was the nickname for mass coined by the Huguenots who had been compelled at the point of the sword to return to the Roman church.

Condé, on the other hand, was far less amenable. So much so that on the evening of September 9th, Charles, furious, swearing and blaspheming more than ever, armed himself from head to foot and announced that he was going to kill 'the rest of the Huguenots' with his own hands, and, 'God's death! he was going to get the Prince de Condé's head first!'

The author of the *Réveille-Matin*, who related the story, added that the young Queen Elizabeth knelt to her husband, imploring him not to do 'a thing of such great moment without the advice of his council'. The King, 'completely convinced by his wife's entreaties, had supper and went to bed with her'. Was this connubial scene, so quickly concluded and ending on the pillows, just a ruse? It is quite probable; for one thing, when the King really lost control and gave way to his lust for blood, it was impossible to lure him back to sanity in this way, while on the other hand it is unlikely that the Queen's charm—though very great—would have wrought such a miracle, as it is well known that he loved elsewhere. Anyhow, if this was mere comedy, it was successful, as Condé was soon compelled to give way in his turn.

A few dates explain the two princes' recantation. In the end, it was Condé who, doubtless for material reasons, was the first to recant in a solemn ceremony held on September 17th, a few days after he had yielded. On the 24th, just one month after the St Bartholomew massacre, the bell of St Germain-l'Auxerrois of sinister memory was pealing for the baptism of Comte de Cheverny's first son. The child 'was held over the font by the Duke of Anjou, the King of Navarre and the Duchess of Lorraine.[2] It was the first baptism in which the King of Navarre was present as a Catholic, which he had become after St Bartholomew's Day'.[3]

Two days later, on the 26th, Henri de Navarre came back to

---

[1] Catherine de Bourbon, Henri's sister, went back to Protestantism and remained a member of the Reformed church until her death, in spite of her brother's entreaties after his own second recantation.

[2] Anjou's sister.

[3] Cheverny, *Mémoires*.

the church to read a long recantation formula forced on 'all those who had lapsed from the Faith and desiring to be received into the Church'.

Finally, on the 29th the Court in its turn was able to enjoy a spectacle: Navarre and Condé, recently brought to heel and accepted into the Order of St Michel, were present as princes and members of the Order at the religious ceremony that was traditional on the feast day of the patron saint of French knighthood. Catherine, seated in the choir, was waiting for her triumph. She stood up when it was Navarre's turn to come and bow to the altar at the offertory. When he passed in front of the ladies he gracefully bowed to them, and the Queen Mother, no longer able to control herself, turned towards the Ambassadors and, in defiance of all the proprieties, burst out laughing.

A few minutes later a messenger, still splashed with mud from the roads along which he had been galloping, crept up to the Queen Mother to give her the news which was to fill her cup of joy to the brim: Longueville was reporting the extermination of the last survivors of Mons. Only one man, La Noue,[1] had escaped. But Catherine was already thinking of making use of his services and of turning his legendary loyalty to good account.

Following the example of Navarre and Condé, a number of Huguenots who had escaped, both in Paris and in the provinces, had agreed to attend Compulsion each Sunday, their lives being well worth it, or their loyalty to their princes compelling them to perjure themselves. Sully, for instance, received a letter from his father, telling him 'he realized he would have to attend mass, as well as his master the King of Navarre and many others, and that he wanted above all that his son should follow the King's fortune to the death, so that he could not be blamed for having forsaken him when he had come on evil days'.[2]

Others had succeeded in crossing the frontiers, often with the help of devout Catholics. They had already reached

---

[1] 1531-1591. One of the outstanding members of the Protestant party. He had fought in most battles and had been very much admired by Coligny. He went back to Flanders in 1578 and at one time was in Alençon's party. He was taken prisoner by Parma and endured arduous imprisonment for several years. When set free at last, he retired for some time to Geneva, then went back to serve Henri IV. He was killed in 1591. He had married Téligny's sister.

[2] Sully, *Mémoires*.

Switzerland, Germany, England, the Channel Islands and even Scandinavia. In spite of approaches by those representing the French Crown in those countries, they had not the slightest desire to go back from exile to face a murderous mob again or put their trust in a bloodthirsty maniac.

Henri Hauser underlines the special importance of the French Protestant emigration. He wrote: 'What gave a world-wide importance to the massacres in France was the fact that they resulted in widespread emigration. One has only to glance at the *Livre des habitants* of Geneva for September and October 1572 and note the hurried, fevered, almost illegible scrawl over the pages, to realize that the secretary was overworked by a tidal wave of Frenchmen who had reached Geneva. It was more or less the same situation at Neuchâtel, Heidelberg, Stuttgart and in England'.[1]

Meanwhile, whole groups of Huguenots had neither recanted nor left France, but they lived in rather special conditions, being entrenched within a few fortified cities like Montauban, Millau, St Antonin, Sancerre, and La Rochelle. The King and his armies would require many months to settle the problem of those Huguenot enclaves by force and negotiation. But that is another story.

On the other hand, the Protestants who could both retain their religion and remain at court were very few. One might have thought that none could do so, had not Sully described a scene which took place on the very day of St Bartholomew: it is worthy of being quoted.

'The King,' wrote Sully, 'drew Ambroise Paré aside, a man whom he greatly loved although he was a Protestant, and told him on St Bartholomew's Day that he must now become a Catholic. The surgeon answered with great courage: "By God's light, Sire, I think you will remember well that you promised there were four things you would never ask me to do, lest I should disobey: go back into my mother's womb, fight in a battle, leave your service, or go to mass".'[2]

Ambroise Paré could probably utter such words: the King knew himself to be grievously ill and that he could not find a better doctor in his kingdom, but one can look in vain for another example of such exceptional pluck.

[1] Hauser, *La prépondérance espagnole*.
[2] Sully, *Mémoires*.

155

An October evening on the Place de Grèves

As a purely arbitrary term to the sequels to St Bartholomew's Day, no scene is more fitting than that which took place in the Place de Grèves in the evening of October 27, 1572.

There, for the last time, were gathered together most of the actors in the tragedy. The King was at a window of the City Hall, hidden behind a curtain (the Queen had been delivered of a daughter that very day); with him were the Queen Mother, their councillors and the whole court, including the newly-converted King of Navarre. On the square below were several thousand men, women and children displaying again that grim look, cruel and bloodthirsty, which the Huguenots had seen during their martyrdom.

And that was really the reason why they were there. The killers had gathered again in order to see two Protestants die. One was a soldier, Briquemault, a redoubtable captain grown grey in the service; the other was a judge, Arnaud de Cavaignes, whom Coligny had wished to be one of the court of enquiry set up to find the arquebusier of August 22nd and the man who had carried out the orders. On the 24th they had both escaped the massacre, and in order to seize them the mob had had to break into the English embassy in the Rue des Bernadins, where Briquemault was hiding, disguised as an ostler, having shaved off his beard and moustache.

Obeying an order given by the King at his bed of justice, Parliament sentenced them both to death for complicity in the Huguenot conspiracy. But neither threats nor torture had made them confess what the King wanted, which would have allowed the ambassadors to repeat the conspiracy fable with some justification. And yet, Briquemault had been weak when faced with death which he had so often faced on the battlefield, and had been ready to cringe to his torturers; he had even offered to betray the plan of the fortifications of La Rochelle, which had been built under his orders. But he knew well that, even if he admitted the existence of a conspiracy, far from saving his life, he would just have made his death more certain. So, after weakening for a moment, he obstinately refused to say what was expected of him. As for Cavaignes, from the beginning to the end of his trial and on the scaffold, he displayed the most unshakeable fortitude, and more courage than the soldier who was sentenced to die with him.

In the dusk, while torches were lit, so that the King could see everything, Briquemault and Cavaignes reached the scaffold. The gallows had been erected in the square. There were three, not two, for by a decision of Parliament a dummy stuffed with straw, looking more or less like Coligny, had been dragged on a hurdle from the conciergerie and was to be delivered to the executioners at the same time as Briquemault and Cavaignes. The effigy had been fitted with the Admiral's clothes and distinctive marks, so that the crowd could recognize it at once. Even the toothpick which Coligny used to chew most of the time during his last years had been remembered. So that, if the Admiral was not there, he was at least represented at this last sinister gathering.

The sentence was read and, so far as Coligny was concerned, it included the most severe provisions ever taken against a condemned man. Not only were his coat of arms and banners to be broken to pieces, and his properties confiscated, but even his children were declared 'ignoble, vile, infamous, incapable of making wills or holding professions, offices, dignity or property in France'. His manor of Chatillon-sur-Loing[1] was to be razed and nothing was ever to be built or erected there; the trees in the park·were to be cut down the middle, and on the ruins a copper plate was to be erected, proclaiming to all who passed the will of the Parliament of Paris.

While the torches smoked and spluttered, the hangman and his assistants strove to keep away the mob which wanted to tear the two men to pieces even before they had been hanged with due ceremony. As for the insatiable Charles IX, he came down to have a close look at the two mutilated bodies and at the grotesque puppet swaying at the ends of their ropes.

Brantôme wrote: 'Some did not find this good, saying that Kings must be cruel only when the circumstances require it, but they should be spectators even less, for fear that they should accustom themselves to the most cruel and inhuman things.' But the King was not interested to know what the historians would say of him. He ended the evening at the City Hall, where the provosts and aldermen had provided a magnificent supper in his honour, with the most costly food and the most intoxi-cating wines.

[1] Now called Chatillon-Coligny.

CHAPTER SEVEN

Historical Perspective

Now that the moment has come to write the last chapter of an historical tale devoted to an event which—then and subsequently—had such political importance as the St Bartholomew Massacre, one is faced with a choice of alternatives. Should one, like so many historians already, pass judgment on the facts, on the protagonists in the drama, or on the drama itself and its consequences and sequels, drawing a conclusion in the full meaning of the word? Or should one rest content with carrying the matter a little farther into time, without comment. Here the choice is very easy: one may even say that it has been made in advance.

Had this book been conceived from the outset as a demonstration, a conclusion would be needed. But this has been, in fact, an attempt at reconstruction, like that of an examining magistrate in a French court—or possibly a restoration, by which an attempt is made to restore life and unity again to an old fresco that has been badly damaged by time and over the centuries has been worked upon by retouchers whose talents cannot excuse their lack of scruple. The workman who puts together the fallen pieces of the fresco or just repaints little bits here and there, is not entitled to turn art critic. If the restoration has been faithful, those for whom it has been done are free to make their own judgment, the only one which really matters. Nevertheless, the task has not been completely carried out if, after having tried to reconstruct the event in its main features and details, one does not take into consideration the verdict passed by intervening centuries.

An impossible estimate

It is often the privilege of the historian to be able to draw up a fairly accurate estimate of an event, a thing which its contemporaries could not always do. In the case of the St Bartholomew massacre, neither those who studied it in the years that followed, nor those who did so centuries later, have ever been able to reckon with any certainty the number of the victims in Paris or the provinces. We can just quote a minimum and a maximum to show how widely different these estimates are.

The least generous author is the Abbé Jean Novi de Caveirac, who in 1758 added a *Dissertation sur la journée de la St Barthélemy* to his *Apologie de Louis XIV sur la Révocation de l'Edit de Nantes*. Caveirac worked in a rather repulsive way on the figures published by Crespin[1] in 1582 and on documents discovered in the Paris archives, especially the sums paid to the grave-diggers. Adding the figures mentioned by Crespin, Caveirac arrived at a total of 6,188 victims for the whole of France, while the author of the *Martyrologe* wrote that 15,138 people had been killed. Then Caveirac found that only 790 of them were mentioned by name. The figure is smaller than the one given by the grave-diggers' accounts for Paris alone—1,100 corpses buried in St Cloud, Auteuil[2] and Chaillot. Yet they did not worry Caveirac, who wrote: 'One may assume that those men who were not refined, either by nature or by trade, did not scruple to swell the number of the buried in order to increase their wages.' The Abbé drew this conclusion: 'Then I think I am going very far when I say that about 1,000 people were killed.' As for the whole of France, after having checked the figures, town by town, and reduced Crespin's calculations to suit his own convenience, Caveirac came to the optimistic conclusion that 'less than 2,000' had been killed. This was all that had perished 'at the most in those unhappy days of horror and mourning'.

At the other extreme we do not find, as might have been expected, a Protestant historian. The highest figure, which seems manifestly exaggerated, unaccountably swollen, was given by a future Archbishop of Paris, Péréfixe, for the benefit of his pupil Louis XIV. Péréfixe, who was not interested in details and who doubtlessly liked round figures, speaks of 100,000 victims.[3] Between Cavierac's 2,000 and Péréfixe's 100,000 almost every figure has been suggested.

[1] Crespin, *Martyrologe des Calvinistes.*
[2] Mostly in the Ile des Cygnes, in the Seine between Passy and Javel. (Translator's note).
[3] Péréfixe, *Vie de Henri le Grand*, published in 1661.

On the Protestant side, the *Tocsin* mentions 2,000 dead for Paris alone, while the *Réveille-Matin* and Simon Goulart speak of 10,000, a figure which has been accepted by the historian Davila. But Sully speaks of 70,000 for the whole of France and de Thou a little less than 30,000. Claude Haton, Chaplain of Notre-Dame de Provins, a contemporary, ultra-catholic writer whose partiality emerges from every page of his account and whose only excuse is the fact that he always lived far from the capital, so that all he knew was by hearsay, mentions 7,000 dead in Paris. He adds that this includes only those whose death was known for certain. As for foreign observers, their estimates are more alike. Petrucci agrees with the English account[1] and with Capilupi when stating that there were 3,000 dead in Paris, while Don Diego de Cuniga, the Spanish Ambassador, gave the same figure, but added that it accounts only for people killed before noon on August 24th.

The wide diversity of figures prevents us from advancing one of our own. One may even wonder on what authority certain historians, confronted with such conflicting evidence, can suggest figures of their own, describing them as 'reasonable' or 'probable'.

Punishment

If it is impossible, after four centuries, to estimate the number of the victims of the massacre with a minimum of historical certainty, it is easier, on the other hand, to discover the fate which attended some of the main characters of the tragedy. It is understandable that Hector de la Ferrière can quote about them the verse from the Gospel according to St Matthew which reads: 'All they that take the sword shall perish with the sword.' It is indeed difficult to find elsewhere in history so many instances of immanent justice striking at so many people guilty of the same collective crime. Of course, the period made it easy, and one might say that so many of the murderers of 1572 died violent deaths because they had lived in the sixteenth century, a time when, despite Hemingway's views, even generals hardly ever died in their beds. . . .

It is well known that Charles IX had but two more years to live, and those two years were haunted by fearful moral and physical suffering. When at last on May 30, 1574, his death

[1] Calendar of State Papers, 1572.

agony began with a 'sweat of blood', he had had the time to expiate the terrible crime which had been forced on him by his mother and brother.

Meanwhile Anjou, his successor, had taken possession of the Polish throne. He rushed back to France, to assume at last the crown he had long coveted, and died sixteen years later, stabbed by a fanatical monk, Jacques Clement, but not without having previously murdered his accomplice of the August days of 1572, Henri de Guise.

Catherine should have been mentioned first: she died two days after Guise. This Queen, who had done so much to make sure that the descendants of the 'Florentine shopkeeper' should reign over France, found perhaps her worst punishment in realizing that, after her beloved son, the crown would go to Henri de Navarre.[1]

Aumale and Angoulême were with Guise on August 24th. The first was killed at La Rochelle by a cannon-ball fired by the Huguenot batteries. The other died by the sword at Aix, fighting a duel against Altovitti, Renée de Châteauneuf's second husband.

As for Bussy d'Amboise, he was compelled by an article of the Peace of La Rochelle in 1573, to return to the heirs of his cousin de Resnel the properties he had stolen. And he was caught by a jealous husband, M. de Montsoreau, who had him murdered by hired assassins, to the benefit of Alexandre Dumas.[2]

Two other principal characters died on the scaffold in the Place de Grèves, decapitated for conspiring against the King: Marc Hannibal de Coconas, a Piedmontese gentleman who had murdered La Force and his son, and La Mole, who had carried the King's secret orders to Provence. And the story goes that two great ladies, who had been their mistresses, the Duchesse de Nevers and Queen Marguerite of Navarre, bought their heads from the hangman and had them embalmed.[3]

At the siege of La Rochelle, two other murderers were killed: Raymond who had been one of La Rochefoucauld's killers, and Cosseins, whose part in the Rue de Bethisy has not been forgotten. After August 24th, Cosseins had been sent to

[1] Her fourth son, Alençon, had died by that time.
[2] And Chapman too: he is the hero of his tragedy *Bussy d'Amboise*.
[3] It has also been made use of by Dumas in his novel, *La Reine Margot*.

Coventry by all the royal officers; despised, and possibly haunted by remorse, he almost seemed to long for death. Brantôme, who saw him shortly before he received the fatal shot, was struck by his sombre expression. When Brantôme asked why he was looking so sad, Cosseins simply answered: 'Cursed be the day of St Bartholomew!'

Maurevert, 'the King's killer', was also at La Rochelle, and he too was scorned and avoided by the other officers, 'who would not even suffer him to be on guard with them'.[1] He emerged from the campaign alive, but died a violent death, nevertheless, a few years later. It was an act of revenge by the son of one of his victims, young de Mouy, who had been after him for a long time and had finally caught up with him one April day in 1583, in the street in front of the church of St Honoré in Paris, running him through with his sword and ripping him open 'from the belly to the left breast'.[2]

Further down the scale one comes to the most repulsive of the murders, Yanowitz, known as Besme. He had been entertained and feasted by Philip II, but on his way back was arrested in Bouteville by the Huguenot garrison. 'Berteville, the Governor of Bouteville, had him imprisoned, while waiting for a decision from the authorities of La Rochelle, who wanted to carry out exemplary justice upon him. He managed to escape, but Berteville was warned in time; he was recaptured and, as he was defending himself, was killed on the spot.'[2]

Finally, another melancholy hero of that bloody tragedy must be mentioned for the prominent part it played: Paris itself. During the years which followed the massacre of St Bartholomew's day, the populace never felt a pang of remorse. Far from it; fired by its preachers, led by various religious orders, it took the most active part in the League, still worshipping the handsome Guise, siding with Spanish intrigues, arming Jacques Clement the regicide monk, and hailing as its king 'Charles X' the Cardinal de Bourbon.

Its attitude was far more political than truly religious. Is it not revealing that a few years after the massacre, city officers in great pomp removed to a church a crucifix which had been hanging for years on the front of a brothel in the Temple district? It was a well-known feature and the people of Paris—

[1] Vicomte de Turenne, duc de Bouillon, *Mémoirs*.
[2] L'Estoile.

good Catholics though they were—always referred to it as the Bawd![1]

In its turn Paris did penance for the massacre. 'On Wednesday, November 1st, All Saints' Day, through a thick fog which cleared as if by a miracle at six in the morning, immediately after the prayers offered at the Pré-aux-Clercs, the King took the faubourg by surprise, where there was great desolation and where poor inhabitants were killed, mostly by M. de Chatillon's men; it was said they remembered that their fathers had been slaughtered by the Parisians, and that as they broke in they shouted: "St Bartholomew! St Bartholomew!" '[1]

This scene took place in 1589, forty days after the battle of Arques. The King of France who forced his way into the faubourgs of Paris was none other than Henri de Bourbon, the little King of Navarre in 1572. And. M de Chatillon, whose troops spread 'death and desolation', was the eldest son of Gaspard de Coligny, Grand Admiral of France.

A wound which took centuries to heal

This very fact, the persistence of hatred for seventeen years after the crime, and a completely reversed situation which provided the sons of the victims with an opportunity to take revenge, on their fathers' behalf, upon the descendants of their murderers, is a proof that the St Bartholomew was more than an error and more than a crime: it was a failure. The Protestant party, deprived of leaders who had somehow come to an arrangement with the King after the Peace of St Germain, took new leaders after the wholesale execution of 1572, men who were singularly less accommodating and in any case less devoted to the King.

The first result of the St Bartholomew was to steel the surviving Protestants, and to widen the gulf between a Huguenot minority and a Catholic majority. On the whole, there was nothing surprising in the fact that, less than twenty years after the massacre, the Protestants kept its name as a war cry. The Parisians, seeing Chatillon's men rushing into the city, did not need to exert their memories to realize the meaning of 'St Bartholomew'. But that took place in 1589.

One might have thought that, with time and the passing of generations and the new events of first magnitude that were

[1] L'Estoile.

added to the calendar of history, the Massacre of St Bartholomew's Day would have been, if not forgotten, yet more or less classified as one of the great crises without which the birth of a nation cannot be achieved. In 1572, no one thought any longer of the violent feuds between Armagnacs and Burgundians.[1] By 1870, the recollection of the Terror[2] and the White Terror[3] no longer divided the French people. Nowadays, we have some difficulty in appreciating how violent was the quarrel over the Commune of 1871[4] and the way it was put down by the Versailles Government. But the St Bartholomew massacre has broken all the rules.

This open wound in France's side in an August night of 1572 has taken more than three centuries to heal. It is true that, periodically, the resurgence of religious quarrels between Catholics and Protestants or free-thinkers, or the unavoidable confusion between religious and political issues, have placed the massacre in the centre of furious discussions. Here are a few examples.

In the years immediately following the massacre, both in France and abroad, a large number of pamphlets on the subject appeared, written in bad verse or in worse prose, in which Protestants and Catholics exchanged insults and accusations. Yet these, like the attack by Chatillon's troops, were done almost in the heat of the event. But it is impossible to plead that excuse for Caveirac's tract, written in 1758 to praise the Revocation of the Edict of Nantes and to compute the number of people killed in the way in which a shopkeeper tries to reduce his stock on stocktaking day. What he wanted to prove was that the number of dead had been grossly exaggerated.

More discussion sprang up when Voltaire, in a note to *La Henriade*, gave proof of the fact that the King had shot at his subjects. This time the St Bartholomew massacre yielded a new argument to conformist people who wanted to abuse that dangerous race of philosophers known as the Encyclopedists.

During the Revolution another aspect of the tragedy was underlined—despite so many events more actual. New arguments against the Monarchy were drawn from this historical

[1] During the Hundred Years War.
[2] In 1793 and 1794.
[3] In 1815, when the Bourbons returned to the throne.
[4] The communist rebellion which took place in Paris after the end of the siege by the Germans, when the Government had retired to Versailles.

example. It was at this time that the plaque was fixed to the Louvre balcony, which was certainly not Charles IX's

In his turn, Bonaparte took part in the fray and had the plaque removed, not because of any historical scruple but because he wanted to stand as a successor to the Capetains rather than take his authority from the Revolutionary assemblies.

With the first years of the Third Republic the time when serious historical research started was reached, but also a time when religious antagonism came to a pitch of new and increased violence.

Historians and scholars started new controversies. Henri Bordier, who brought so many new documents to light, thought it was 'humiliating for the country and for science to have to fight for the theses put up by de Thou, against lies concocted by willing accomplices and the nonsense of so-called impartial scholars who pretend to be above partisan passion'. More or less at the same time, from the other side of the fence, the *Société générale de librairie catholique* published a biography of Coligny in which the author made his purpose quite clear: 'I got the idea of this long research when some people had the strange idea of erecting a statue to Coligny,[1] a man who betrayed his God, his King and his country.'[2]

Such quarrels reached beyond scholars and the lecture-rooms of the Sorbonne. Bordier quoted, with full references, a literary exercise given to pupils of a religious school in 1878. It ran thus: 'Charles IX and the great Catherine de Medici will always be dear to the heart of the true Christians. Thanks to their courage and heroic faith, the country was rid of 50,000 Huguenots in one night.'[3]

Only at the beginning of the present century did the massacre of 1572 cease to divide the French people. It is enough to reveal the extraordinary influence that such a collective crime, brought about mostly by fanaticism and intolerance, had over the conscience of a whole nation, through several centuries.

Now the massacre of St Bartholomew's Day is no longer a theme for polemics. May it be, for those who have a faith, a cause for reflection!

[1] It was erected against the apse of the Oratoire, the main Protestant church in Paris. The sculptor was Crauk.

[2] Charles Buet. *L'Amiral de Coligny.*

[3] *Journal du XIXe siècle*, March 27, 1879, p. 2, col. 1 (quoted by H. Bordier).

INDEX

Acier, Seigneur d', 123n
Albret, Jeanne d', 23, 117
Alençon, Duke of, 18, 26, 105–6, 129
Alva, Duke of, 16, 41, 50
Amboise, Bussy d', 99, 108, 161
Amboise conspiracy, 21–2
Angoulême, Chevalier d', 25; feud with Coligny, 71, 80, 82–3; role in Massacre, 91, 93; death, 161
Anjou, Henri Duke of, 18, 26, 101; Catherine's favourite, 27, 28; Charles jealous of, 42; plots Coligny's death, 45, 52, 56; at Tuileries meeting, 58–9; Catherine's accomplice, 65, 66; the Discours, 66–7, 69, 78–9; jealous of Condé, 70; murdered Guise, 123n; death, 161
Aubigné, Agrippa d', 102
Aumale, Duke of: stays in Paris, 54–5, 57; present at Coligny's murder, 71, 80, 82; role in Massacre, 91, 93, 122; death, 161

Barnaud, Nicolas, 46n, 103n
Barrère, Joseph, 103
Bayancourt, see Bouchavannes
'Beggars' Revolt', 16–17
Birague, René de, 45, 50, 58
Biron, Marshal de, 124, 133
Bordier, Henri, 103
Boussuet, J. B., 103
Bouchavannes (Bayancourt), Seigneur de, 54n, 60, 66, 88
Bourbon, House of, 23, 69–70
Bourges, 140
Brantôme, Seigneur de, 103, 105, 157
Brion, Seigneur de, 89n, 90
Briquemault, Capt., 60, 156–7

Calvinism, 14–15; in France, 20
Catherine de Bourbon, 152, 153n
Catherine de' Medici, 16, 18; regent, 21–2; character, 23–7; jealous of Coligny, 31; decides to use the Guises, 31; plans Coligny's death, 40–5, 48; Charles turns on, 51–2, 55–6, 63; alleges Huguenot plot, 65–6; on the eve, 73–4, 78–80; on the day, 84, 104–6; letters to provinces, 119–21; traduces Coligny, 129–30; letter to Strozzi, 135–6; death, 161
Catherine of Cleves, 33
Cavaignes, Arnaud de, 52, 156–7
Caveirac, Abbé de, 159, 164
Certon, Salomon, 76, 81n
Chailly, Seigneur de, 46, 50, 55
Chamont, 74, 76, 90–1
Charles IX, King of France: collusion with William of Orange, 17; becomes king, 21; jealous of Anjou, 27; character, 27–

30; adopts Coligny as adviser, 27, 30–1; reaction to attack on Coligny, 48–50; rebukes Catherine, 51–2; accuses the Guises, 53–4; duped, 56–7, 63–6; 'Kill them all!', 67–8, 71, 88, 108; turns on Navarre, 84–5; shot Huguenots? 102–4; gloats over the dead, 105, 132, 157; appoints City Council, 131–2; takes full responsibility, 136–7; letters to provinces, 137–8; betrays survivors of Mons, 145–7; death, 160–1
Charpentier, 114–5
Chartres, Vidame de, 51n, 93, 151
Chatillon, see Coligny
Clermont, see Piles
Coconas, Comte Mark-Hannibal de, 117, 133, 161
Coligny, Admiral Gaspard de (Seigneur de Chatillon), 23; influence on Charles, 27, 31; feud with the Guises, 32–4; career, 34–6, 39–40; Maurevert's attack, 40–52; murder, 81–3, 96; his children, 128–9, 163; posthumous attacks, 129–30, 157
Condé, Prince Henri de: reaction to Maurevert's attempt, 48–9, 51; life spared, 69, 70n; defies Charles, 84–5, 106; recants, 152–4
Condé, Prince Louis de, 22–3, 41
Condé, Princesse de, see Marie de Clèves
Cornaton, 46, 56, 81
Cossé, Marshal de, 29, 50, 124
Cosseins, Col., 56, 60, 80, 82; death, 161–2
Crucé (Thomas), 115–6

Damville, Marshal de, 49, 50
Diane de Poitiers, 25, 58–9
Dijon, 138, 143–4
Discours d'un personnage d'honneur et de qualité, 42n, 66–7, 69
Dumas, Alexandre, 161n

Ecouen, Edict of, 20–1
Edict of Pacification, 35, 43, 44, 50, 120, 138
Elizabeth I, Queen of England, 17–18, 150–1
Elizabeth of Austria, Queen of France, 29–30, 105, 153
Englishmen, treatment of, 100–1, 114
Este, Anne d', 32–3, 42–4

Ferrier, Jean, 116
Fizes, Simon de, 54
Fleming, Jane, 25
'Flying Squadron' (Catherine's maids of honour), 54, 104–5

166